ABOUT THE PUBLISHER

New York Institute of Finance

. . . more than just books.

NYIF offers practical, applied training and education in a wide range of formats and topics:

* *Classroom training:* evenings, mornings, noon-hours
* *Seminars and conferences:* one-, two-, and three-day introductory, intermediate-, and professional-level programs
* *Customized training:* need-specific programs conducted on your site or ours; in New York City, throughout the United States, anywhere in the world
* *Independent study:* self-paced learning—basic, intermediate, or advanced
* *Exam preparation:* NASD licensing (including Series 3, 6, 7, 24, 27, 63); C.F.A.; state life and health insurance

Subjects of books and training programs include the following:

* Account Executive Training
* Brokerage Operations
* Currency Trading
* Futures Trading
* International Corporate Finance
* Investment Analysis
* Options Trading
* Securities Transfer
* Selling Securities
* Technical Analysis
* Treasury Management
* Yield Curve Analysis

When Wall Street professionals think **training**, *they think NYIF.*

For further information, please call or write to us. Please specify your areas of interest—classroom training, custom programs, independent-study courses, exam preparation, or books—so that we can respond promptly to your inquiry.

New York Institute of Finance
70 Pine Street
New York, NY 10270–0003
212 / 344–2900
FAX: 212 / 514-8423
TELEX: 238790

Simon & Schuster, Inc. A Gulf + Western Company

"Where Wall Street Goes to School" ™

Trading Stocks on the Over-the-Counter Market

New York Institute of Finance

Library of Congress Cataloging-in-Publication Data

Trading stocks on the over-the-counter market / by NYIF staff.
p. cm.
Includes index.
ISBN 0-13-926007-2 : $21.50
1. Over-the-counter markets--United States. I. New York Institute of Finance.
HG4910.T7 1988
322.64'3'0973--dc19 88-29378
CIP

This publication is designed to provide accurate and authoritative information in regard to the subject matter covered. It is sold with the understanding that the publisher is not engaged in rendering legal, accounting, or other professional service. If legal advice or other expert assistance is required, the services of a competent person should be sought.

From a Declaration of Principles Jointly Adopted by a Committee of the American Bar Association and a Committee of Publishers and Associations

A Division of Simon & Schuster, Inc.
70 Pine Street
New York, NY 10270-0003

Printed in the United States of America

10 9 8 7 6 5 4 3 2 1

New York Institute of Finance
(NYIF Corp.)
70 Pine Street
New York, New York 10270-0003

CHAPTER 2
Getting the Most from Your OTC Investments

CHAPTER 3
Choosing Substantial OTC Stocks for Investment

CHAPTER 5
Managing Your Own Investment Program or Leaving It to the Pros

CHAPTER 6
The OTC Marketplace: Life After October 19

APPENDIX I
Investment Publications Particularly Relevant to the Over-the-Counter Market

APPENDIX II
The Functioning of the NASD

APPENDIX *III* Financial Statement Analysis

APPENDIX *IV*
Obtaining Redress If You Feel You Have Been Defrauded

Index

Introduction

The Over-the-Counter Market: Last Investment Frontier for the Individual

Recent studies indicate that approximately thirty million Americans own stock, with that number growing daily. But for many investors the ownership of stock is restricted to household names such as AT&T and IBM—stocks traded on the major exchanges. However, investing exclusively in listed stocks deprives investors of the opportunities available over the counter, in what might be called the last investment frontier wide open to the individual investor.

The listed market is closely followed and constantly reevaluated by professional and institutional investors and, for the most part, the assets and/or growth potential of listed companies are fully priced. In many instances individual investors can earn a greater return and express their own individual investment style by trading in the over-the-counter market. Here, as opposed to the listed market, the individual investor is on an equal footing with—and may even have an advantage over—the market professional. Because the individual investor does not have to report to clients who are comfortable only with "known" stocks and who expect instant performance, an individual investor can buy selected over-the-counter stocks when they are cheap and sell them at a higher price later, when they have been discovered by the market professionals.

The diversity of OTC stocks also provides an opportunity for the individual. What kinds of stocks are traded in this market? Companies with substantial assets, earnings, and capitalization, that is, blue chips, represent one example. At the other end of the spectrum are penny stocks, the so-called cats and dogs of the investment world. New issues are also traded over the counter and these range from substantial companies to start-up issues that may represent real growth opportunities. Less well-known categories of OTC stocks include the stocks of bankrupt companies, those of regional smokestack companies, and the stocks of banks and insurance companies. Stocks of international companies are also traded over the counter.

Many institutions and professionals are precluded by law from investing in stocks of some of these categories of companies, so these fields are wide open to the astute investor who can recognize undiscovered value in OTC stocks. This diversity of opportunity can prove interesting and financially rewarding to you, as an individual investor—whether you are looking for more conservative opportunities or prefer investments with a higher risk in exchange for potentially greater return.

For a number of reasons, individual investors have in the past been hesitant to buy stocks traded over the counter. This reluctance often stems from a lack of knowledge about this marketplace. This book is intended to provide the information you, as an individual investor, need to make the most of the opportunities available over the counter. The first chapter takes you "inside the marketplace" and describes for you how the OTC marketplace functions. The chapter then goes on to discuss some of the traditional objections to investing there. Many of these objections have been eliminated by improvements in the marketplace, such as the institution of NASDAQ and the oversight of the NASD. Other objections, such as the claim that the OTC market is illiquid, can be overcome simply by the investor's having adequate knowledge about the liquidity of particular stocks. Other objections are shown to be just plain myth.

Beyond general market information, you need strategies and techniques for making your OTC investments work. To avoid pitfalls you need to understand the "rules of the game." The material included in Chapter 2 shows you how to be a "smart" investor in the OTC market: How to choose a broker, what signals to look for with regard to particular stocks (float and spread, for example), and whether to trade on margin are examples of the types of information covered in this chapter.

Chapters 3 and 4 get down to the nitty-gritty of stock picking. Knowing the rules of the game and the strategies of OTC investing won't bring success unless you pick the right stocks at the right time. These chapters describe each of the categories of OTC stocks in detail and present principles for choosing those categories that are appropriate for your investment goals and risk tolerance. Lists of representative stocks for consideration are also included.

Different OTC stocks work differently and are evaluated on different bases. Some types require considerable number crunching, while others are evaluated primarily in terms of sponsorship or on the basis of personal knowledge of an industry. Chapters 3 and 4 also show you which analytical tools to emphasize in your analysis of different types of stocks. A more rigorous treatment of what the specific ratios represent and how the particulars of financial analysis are applied is included in Appendix III.

Chapter 5 acknowledges that some investors have both the time and inclination to manage their own investment programs, while others do not. Whatever your investment style, there are opportunities for you in the OTC market. For investors who like to pick their own stocks, this chapter discusses where to find investment ideas, how to keep track of financials, how to use personal contacts, and how to approach a company's management. For investors who prefer professional management, the chapter covers some representative types of funds that invest heavily in the OTC market. These mutual funds are explored in terms of their investment philosophies so that you can choose those that are consistent with your own approach.

Finally, Chapter 6 discusses an event that weighs on the thinking of all investors: the October 18, 1987 market break. How was the OTC market affected? How well has it recovered? The chapter also shows you what improvements were implemented in the OTC marketplace in response to the problems that surfaced on October 19.

The material in these chapters is designed to enable the individual investor to function comfortably in the OTC marketplace. Whether you are a novice investor or a seasoned stock trader who is new to the over-the-counter market, this book can help you separate the fact from the fiction about OTC investing. The investor who has already ventured into the OTC market can find sound strategies and a sensible and personally appropriate approach to developing an investment program and to choosing particular stocks.

The material in the chapters presents an overview and is developed along the lines of basic investment principles. However, the book can also serve as a reference source. Appendix I contains a list and descriptions of investment publications/advisory services and their addresses and prices at the time of this writing. In addition, the appendixes include detailed material on the workings of the National Association of Securities Dealers (Appendix II); financial analysis (Appendix III); and particulars regarding transactions, settlement, delivery, and regulations. Appendix IV describes the procedures for obtaining redress if you feel you have been treated unfairly.

The OTC marketplace represents both a challenge and an opportunity for you, the individual investor. The diversity of OTC-traded companies presents a challenge in that you need to be able to understand and evaluate a variety of different stocks—not just the household name, "blue-chip" type stocks typically listed on the exchanges. On the other hand, the OTC market offers you an opportunity in that here you are on an equal footing with the institutional investor. As an individual investor in the OTC market, you need not be concerned with program trading and portfolio insurance and the volatility that accompanies them. If you use the information and techniques presented in this book you should be able to identify undervalued and growth situations among the thousands of stocks traded over the counter.

1

Understanding the Over-the-Counter Marketplace

May 17, 1792 is a landmark date in securities trading in the United States: On that day, twenty-four of New York City's leading merchants and businessmen agreed to trade stocks only among themselves and to adhere to agreed-on commission rates. This agreement marked the founding of the New York Stock Exchange (NYSE), perhaps the most significant organized location for buying and selling stocks.

However, not all stocks are eligible for trading on the NYSE. Even in the early years, companies were required to meet certain standards in order to be listed for trading on the New York Stock Exchange, the American Stock Exchange, or any of the regional exchanges that came into existence. To be listed, a company had to have a certain amount of assets and earnings and a minimum number of shareholders. As time passed these standards became more stringent.

So, you might ask, how did stocks trade before the exchanges were opened? And how do the stocks of those companies that either do not meet the exchanges' listing requirements or that do not wish to list with an exchange trade? Originally, they were traded physically "over the counter" in the offices of the many investment bankers that sprang up to meet businesses' need for growth capital. Nowadays transactions in such stocks are generally executed over the telephone but the term *over the counter* (OTC) has remained to describe the manner of buying and selling securities anywhere but on a registered exchange.

A comparison of the way in which over-the-counter and listed securities trade reveals a number of differences and similarities. To make such a comparison meaningful to you, this chapter describes the trading processes in both arenas, highlighting such concepts as the difference between a negotiated and an auction marketplace, the role of the market maker versus that of the specialist, and the "players" (the persons who actually get the trades done) in the respective marketplaces. Also in this chapter you get a chance to examine some of the traditional objections to and myths about the OTC market to determine whether they indeed reflect the truth.

HOW A STOCK IS TRADED OVER THE COUNTER

The OTC market has no centralized location for the conduct of business; buyers and sellers must seek each other out. A typical OTC transaction might take place as follows:

Joe Investor is seeking to buy 100 shares of ABC, an unlisted stock, at the best possible price. He calls Mary Broker, who writes an order ticket. The ticket is sent to an OTC trader in the firm, John Trader, who then must find a broker willing to sell 100 shares of ABC. Normally such a broker is a *market maker* in ABC; that is, someone who provides bids and offerings for that particular security on an ongoing basis.

To find a market maker, John Trader might look to the daily *pink sheets* of the National Quotation Bureau Inc. (NQB), a private publisher of financial information. The pink sheets, so-called because they are printed on pink paper, list in alphabetical order approximately 20,000 over-the-counter stocks along with the names of market makers in those stocks and the previous day's bids and offers quotations. If ABC is an actively traded stock, there may be several market makers listed in the pink sheets. John Trader begins by calling the competing market makers to learn their current prices for the stock and establish a basis for negotiation. He then contacts any number of the market makers to try to negotiate the best possible price for his client. When he finds the market maker who agrees to sell 100 shares of ABC at the lowest price, he executes the transaction.

Alternatively, if John Trader's firm subscribes to the National Association of Securities Dealers Automated Quotations (NASDAQ) and if ABC is listed on the NASDAQ system, he can go to the NASDAQ computer terminal, or Quotron machine, and find the current quotations of NASD members who make a market in ABC. He can also find information about volume and price range for the preceding week. Because NASDAQ quotations are continuously updated, John Trader does not need to make an initial series of requests for current quotations; he can instantly find the market maker with the best price and negotiate with him or her immediately.

Figure 1–1 shows a page drawn from the pink sheets. Note that the quotes are listed in alphabetical order by company name and that some stocks show as few as one market maker while others have fifteen or more. Also note that some of the stocks listed in the pink sheets have four-letter symbols next to their names, indicating that they are traded on NASDAQ, as well as via the "sheets."

Symbols such as VJ, BW, and OW appear next to certain of the stocks. The symbol VJ means that the particular company is in bankruptcy. (This type of stock is discussed extensively in Chapter 4.) The symbols BW ("bid wanted") and OW ("offer wanted") mean, respectively, that the market maker is soliciting a bid for stock held or is requesting to be shown or offered stock. When both a bid and asked price are shown the market is referred to as a *two-sided market,* that is, the market maker is holding itself out to purchase at least 100 shares at the bid price and sell at least 100 shares at the offer price.

FIGURE 1–1. Sample Page Drawn from the Pink Sheets.

STOCK	PAGE 101	NOV. 13,1987		NATIONAL DAILY QUOTATION SERVICE		
VJ ENCHANTED VLG INC 10 PR A		REICH & CO INC NY	800 221 7468			
		MAYER&SCHWEITZER INC J CY	800 631 3094			
		HERZOG HEINE GEDULD NY	800 327 7022			
		NASH WEISS & CO INC J CY	800 526 3041			
VJ ENCHANTED VILLAGE INC		NASH WEISS & CO INC J CY	800 526 3041			
		GREENTREE SECS CORP NY	212 968 9620			
		MAYER&SCHWEITZER INC J CY	800 631 3094			
		HERZOG HEINE GEDULD NY	800 327 7022			
		TROSTER SINGER CORP J CY	800 222 0890			
VJ ENCHANTED VILLAGE INC A		HERZOG HEINE GEDULD NY	800 327 7022			
		NASH WEISS & CO INC J CY	800 526 3041			
		MAYER&SCHWEITZER INC J CY	800 631 3094			
VJ ENCHANTED VILLAGE 91 WTS		NASH WEISS & CO INC J CY	800 526 3041			
		MAYER&SCHWEITZER INC J CY	800 631 3094			
		HERZOG HEINE GEDULD NY	800 327 7022			
		REICH & CO INC NY	800 221 7468			
ENCINO SVGS&LN ASSN GTEE		J ALEXANDER SECS INC LA	800 421 0258			
		BATEMAN EICHLER HR INC SF	800 227 3207			
ENCO PRODUCTS INC		TROSTER SINGER CORP J CY	800 222 0890			
M- ENCOR ENERGY CORP	EECIF	WK VOL- N/A HB- N/A	LB- N/A	4 3/8	4 7/8	
		FBCO,SAXP				
M- ENCORE COMPUTER CORP	ENCC	WK VOL- 2171 HB- 2 3/4	LB- 2 1/4	2 5/8	2 3/4	
		CHIC,FAHN,HMQT,HRZG,KPCO,MASH,MOKE,MOTC				
		NAWE,PWJC,SAXP,SHWD,SUMM,TMSI,TREE,TSCO				
		VINR,WIEN				
VJ ENCORE INDUS INC		DATEK SECS CORP NY	212 785 6000			
ENDATA INC COM		JB RICHARDS SECS CRP CHGO	800 621 5253			
		LOEB PARTNERS NY	212 483 7343			
VJ ENDO LASE INC COM		NASH WEISS & CO INC J CY	800 526 3041			
		TROSTER SINGER CORP J CY	800 222 0890			
		REICH & CO INC NY	800 221 7468			
		HERZOG HEINE GEDULD NY	800 221 3600			
VJ ENDOTRONICS INC	ENDQC	WK VOL- 330 HB- 5/16	LB- 1/4	5/16	7/16	
		CHIC,DAIN,HRZG,KINN,MASH,NAWE,SHWD,SUMM				
		TRFE				
ENER-MARK CORP	ENMK	WK VOL- 100 HB- 3/32	LB- 1/16	3/32	5/32	
		CARR,DARB,FRAN,HILL,SHWD,STCO,TSCO				
		INVESTORS ASSOCS HACK NJ	800 222 0282			
ENERCO INC		NEIDIGER TUCKER BRNR DENV	800 525 3086			
		NASH WEISS & CO INC J CY	800 526 3041			
		GREENTREE SECS CORP NY	800 547 7070			
ENERCOMP INC COM		TROSTER SINGER CORP J CY	800 222 0890			
		CARR SECS CORP NY	800 221 2243			
ENERCORP INC		BLINDER ROBINSN&CO ENGLWD	800 525 2344			
		ALLIED CAPITAL GRP ENGLWD	303 790 2480			
ENERDYNE CORP COM		CARR SECS CORP NY	800 221 2243			
		SHERWOOD SECS CORP NY	800 525 3499			
M- ENERGAS CO	EGAS	WK VOL- 213 HB- 12 1/2	LB- 12 1/8	13 3/8	13 5/8	
		DEAN,EHUT,HDLY,KPCO,MOTC,SPHN,TMSI,WERT				
ENERGETICS INC 1.80 PR 1		CARR SECS CORP NY	800 221 2243	OW		
ENERGETICS INC	EJTX	WK VOL- 186 HB- 5/32	LB- 5/32	5/32	3/16	
		CARR,CONE,GILS,MCHO,RMSI,SHWD,TSCO				
		MULLER & CO NY	800 233 0764			
		NASH WEISS & CO INC J CY	800 526 3041			
		CARR SECS CORP NY	800 221 2243			
ENERGEX CORP		GREENTREE SECS BOCA RATON	800 327 5000			
		MONARCH FUNDING CORP NY	212 406 4047			
		COVEY & CO INC SLC	800 453 5737			
ENERGEX MINERALS LTD	EGEXF	WK VOL- 83 HB- 1/2	LB- 7/16	1/2	5/8	
		CARR,FITZ,HRZG,MRKS,NAWE,RSNY,SHWD,TIMM				
		TREE				
		FITZGERALD DEARMN&R TULSA	800 527 1746			
		NASH WEISS & CO INC J CY	800 526 3041			
		CARR SECS CORP NY	800 221 2243			
ENERGRO INC		DILLON SECS INC NY	800 622 6602			
		EQUITY SECS TRDG CO MNPLS	800 328 4598			
ENERGROUP TECHNOLOGIES		FITZGERALD DEARMN&RBT SLC	800 223 6379	1/8	1/2	
		GREENTREE SECS BOCA RATON	800 327 5000			
		WIEN SECURITIES CORP J CY	800 624 0050			
		NASH WEISS & CO INC J CY	800 526 3041			
ENERGY ACQUISITIONS INC		GENERAL BND&SHARE CO DENV	303 733 8437	OW		UNS
ENERGY ASSETS INTL CORP	EAIC	WK VOL- 465 HB- 5/8	LB- 7/16	5/8	3/4	
		BUSI,CARR,HRZG,MHMY,NAWE,SHWD,TSCO,WHCC				
ENERGY CAPITAL DEV CORP	ECDC	WK VOL- 22 HB- 1 3/4	LB- 1 3/4	1 3/4	2 1/2	
		CARR,DILN,NAWE				
ENERGY CO OF NORTH AMER		CARR SECS CORP NY	800 221 2243			
M- ENERGY CONVERSION DEV COM	ENER	WK VOL- 2090 HB- 11 3/4	LB- 9 1/2	10	10 1/4	
		ALLN,BEHR,BEST,BLAR,HRZG,MOTC,OPCO,PIPR				

FIGURE 1–1. Sample Page Drawn from the Pink Sheets (cont'd.).

		SAXP,TMSI,TSCO,VINF,WEDB,WERT			
ENERGY CVRSN DEV 91 WTS	ENERW	WK VOL- 411 HB- 5/8	LB- 3/8	1/2	3/4
		BEST,HRZG,OPCO,PIPR			
ENERGY CVRSN DEV 92UTS WI	ENERU	WK VOL- N/A HB- 12	LB- 11	11	16
		ALLN,BEST,HRZG			
ENERGY CVRSN DEV INC92WTS	ENERL	WK VOL- 11 HB- 2	LB- 2	2	4
		ALLN,BEST,HRZG			
ENERGY DYNAMICS INTL CORP		DATEK SECS CORP NY	212 785 6000		
VJ ENERGY EXCHANGE CRP A COM		TROSTER SINGER CORP N MMI	800 327 7001		
		CARR SECS CORP NY	800 221 2243		
N- ENERGY FACTORS INC COM	EFAC	WK VOL- 1327 HB- 6	LB- 5 1/4	6	6 1/4
		BEHR,DEAN,EHUT,HRZG,MOTC,RODR,SAXP,SELZ			
		SHWD,TSCO,TUCK,WIEN			
		LF ROTHSCHILD&CO INC NY	212 248 2722		
ENERGY INTL OVERSEAS CORP		CARR SECS CORP NY	800 221 2243		
VJ ENERGY MNGMT CORP 10 PR A		CARR SECS CORP NY	800 221 2243		
		J T MORAN & CO NY	212 363 6095		
VJ ENERGY MANAGEMENT CORP		CARR SECS CORP NY	800 221 2243		
		J T MORAN & CO NY	212 363 6095		
ENERGY MINERALS CORP		MAYER&SCHWEITZER INC J CY	800 631 3094		
ENERGY MOTOR CONTROL INC		HILL THMPSN MAGID&CO J CY	800 631 3083		
		WIEN SECURITIES CORP J CY	800 624 0050		BW
		TROSTER SINGER CORP J CY	800 222 0890		
ENERGY OPTICS INC		YOUNG SMITH&PEACOCK PHNX	800 528 0320		
		SHERWOOD SECS CORP NY	800 435 1235		
		J T MORAN &CO SHRWSBRY NJ	800 542 2843		
		NASH WEISS & CO INC J CY	800 526 3041		
		GREENTREE SECS BOCA RATON	800 327 5000		
		TROSTER SINGER CORP J CY	800 222 0890		
		LEGG MASON WOOD WALKER NY	212 428 4949		
		HILL THMPSN MAGID&CO J CY	800 631 3083		
		CHAPIN DAVIS & CO BALT	800 334 9950		
		J T MORAN &CO SHRWSBRY NJ	201 542 9090		
ENERGY PRODUCTION CO COM		DATEK SECS CORP NY	212 785 6000		
		CARR SECS CORP NY	800 221 2243		
ENERGY RECOVERY SYS COM		NASH WEISS & CO INC J CY	800 526 3041		
		TROSTER SINGER CORP J CY	800 222 0890		
		GREENTREE SECS CORP NY	212 968 9620		
		M H MEYERSON &CO INC J CY	212 425 1212	.02	.05
		M RIMSON & CO INC NY	800 221 4934		
		F N WOLF & CO INC NY	212 635 5686		
		WIEN SECURITIES CORP J CY	800 624 0050		
		M H MEYERSON &CO INC J CY	800 333 3113	.02	.05
		SHERWOOD SECS CORP NY	800 435 1235		
		P R HERZIG & CO NY	212 606 5771		
ENERGY RESERVE INC		FINCL AMERICA SECS CLEVE	800 321 0550		
		WIEN SECURITIES CORP J CY	800 624 0050		
		KIDDER PEABODY & CO LA	800 421 8047	2 3/4	3 1/4
		HERZOG HEINE GEDULD NY	800 221 3600		
		NASH WEISS & CO INC J CY	800 526 3041		
		GREENTREE SECS CORP NY	212 968 9620		
		TROSTER SINGER CORP J CY	800 222 0890		
		SHERWOOD SECS CORP NY	800 435 1235		
		HILL THMPSN MAGID&CO J CY	800 631 3083		
ENERGY RESERVES GROUP INC		GREENTREE SECS CORP NY	212 968 9620		
		WEDBUSH SECS INC NY	212 422 0011	5 1/2	
		BLUMENTHAL SECS INC NY	212 308 4206		
		MAYER&SCHWEITZER INC J CY	800 631 3094		
ENERGY RES OF N D	SAVE	WK VOL- 4 HB- 7/8	LB- 1/2	1/2	1
		CARR,HILL,KINN			
ENERGY SCIENCES CORP		EMMETT A LARKIN CO INC SF	800 227 4545		
ENERGY SVC CO INC 89 WTS		DOFT & CO INC NY	212 483 1976		
		PRESCOTT BALL&TURBEN CLEV	800 323 6895		
		BEAR STEARNS & CO NY	800 221 2852		
		F P QUINN TRADING CO NY	212 751 4443		
		MERRILL LYNCH PFS NY	212 449 4037		
ENERGY SHED INC		DATEK SECS CORP NY	212 785 6000		
ENERGY SOLUTIONS INC		DATEK SECS CORP NY	212 785 6000		
		SHERWOOD SECS CORP NY	800 435 1235		
		MULLER & CO NY	800 233 0764		
		HERZOG HEINE GEDULD NY	800 221 3600		
		WIEN SECURITIES CORP J CY	800 624 0050		BW
		NASH WEISS & CO INC J CY	800 526 3041		
ENERGY SOURCES INC		TROSTER SINGER CORP N MMI	800 327 7001		
		CARR SECS CORP NY	800 221 2243		
		WEDBUSH SECS INC LA	800 421 0153		
ENERGY SYS HLDGS LTD ORD		NASH WEISS & CO INC J CY	800 526 3041		
		HERZOG HEINE GEDULD NY	800 221 3600		

STOCK PAGE 101 NOV. 13,1987 NATIONAL DAILY QUOTATION SERVICE

Finally, note that for some of the stock listed in Figure 1–1, only the names of broker/dealers or abbreviations for their names are shown. Such a stock is referred to as listed in *name only*. By entering such a quote, the particular market making firm requires any interested party to contact it for an actual quote. In other words, the market maker is unwilling to put a specific quote in the sheets for the stock.

The Role of the Market Maker

The foregoing paragraphs should give you a grasp of at least the basic terminology of the over-the-counter marketplace. Your familiarity with the jargon of the over-the-counter market will grow, the more OTC stocks you buy and sell. But more important than a grasp of the jargon is an understanding of the role played by market makers in the way OTC stocks are traded. As you will see later in this chapter, market makers perform much of the same function as specialists on the exchanges.

As described in the example on page 8, when John Trader wants to execute the purchase of ABC for his client, he contacts a market maker in ABC. How does a firm become a market maker in a particular stock?

Becoming a Market Maker. First, a broker/dealer must be registered with the U.S. Securities & Exchange Commission (SEC), the federal agency created in 1934 to regulate the nation's financial markets. Although only registered broker/dealers can function as market makers in the over-the-counter market, not all registered broker/dealers function as such. A firm becomes a market maker because it has an interest in making a market in a particular stock. This interest may stem from a number of factors:

- A brokerage firm that takes a company public may feel a responsibility to maintain a liquid market for its stock.
- A brokerage firm may see other market makers quoting the stock and feel that it too could trade in it profitably.

- The stock may have been brought to the attention of the broker/dealer by an investor or corporate officer interested either in creating a market for the company's stock or in increasing the number of market makers to add to the stock's liquidity.

Figure 1–2 shows a sample of the listing application a firm must file with the National Quotation Bureau, Inc. in order to have its quotes for a particular issue listed in the pink sheets. As you can see from the sample listing application, a broker/dealer who makes a market in a stock must have available detailed, up-to-date financials on the company. (The company's financials must be current and its filing with the SEC up to date.) The prospective market maker agrees to take on the responsibility of maintaining a *due diligence file* on the company, including such things as current financials, press releases, and articles about the company. In this way the market maker acknowledges a responsibility to keep current with the activity of any company it makes a market in. If a broker/dealer is not trying to list a new stock in the pink sheets, but rather is seeking to become a market maker in a stock already quoted there, the full listing application containing company financials is not required. However, the market making firm must still maintain a due diligence file.

Types of Market Makers

OTC market makers are basically of two types. First, there are the so-called *wholesale market makers*, including such brokerage firms as Carr Securities, Inc. and Troster Singer, Inc., to name just two. Such firms deal exclusively with other broker/dealers and for the most part have no retail customers. These firms are frequently referred to as brokers' brokers and make their profits from their trading ability, that is, their ability to buy low and sell high. The second and more common type of market maker, often called a *retail market maker*, is the brokerage firm that makes a market in stocks but also carries out a number of other investment banking and financial service functions. For the most part, this type of broker/dealer

FIGURE 1–2. Listing Application for the National Quotation Bureau, Inc.

National Quotation Bureau incorporated

No quotation will be published until the broker-dealer seeking to insert the quotation furnishes the information requested in Parts 1 and 2 below, and if necessary, the information in Part 3, and duly executes and delivers this form.

PART 1

A. Exact name of the issuer and predecessor (if any).

B. State of incorporation.

C. Address of principal executive offices.

D. Complete title and class of security to be quoted.

E. Par or stated value of security.

F. Name and address of any transfer agent.

G. Number of shares outstanding of the security as of the end of the issuer's most recent fiscal year.

H. Price at which security is to be initially quoted. Bid______________Asked____________

PART 2

Check the item below which indicates the exemption from Rule 15c2-11 of the Securities Exchange Act of 1934 (the "34 Act") upon which you rely in submitting your quotation.

☐ A. The issuer has filed a registration statement under the Securities Act of 1933 (the "33 Act") which became effective less than 90 calendar days prior to the date hereof, and such registration statement has not been the subject of a stop order which is still in effect, and the undersigned has in its records a copy of the prospectus specified by Section 10(a) of the 33 Act; or

☐ B. The issuer has filed a notification under Regulation A of the 33 Act which became effective less than 40 calendar days prior to the date hereof, and the offering circular provided for under Regulation A has not become the subject of a suspension order which is still in effect, and the undersigned has in his records a copy of such offering circular; or

☐ C. (i) The issuer is required to file reports pursuant to Section 13 or 15d of the 34 Act, or is an issuer of a security covered by Section 12(g) (2) (B) or (G) of the 34 Act; and

(ii) the undersigned has a reasonable basis for believing the issuer is current in filing the reports required to be filed at regular intervals pursuant to Section 13 or 15d of the 34 Act, or, in the case of insurance companies, exempted from Section 12(g) of the 34 Act by subparagraph 12(g) (2) (G) thereof, the annual statement referred to in Section 12(g) (2) (G) (i) of the 34 Act; and

(iii) the undersigned has in his records the issuer's most recent annual report (on Form 10-K) filed pursuant to Section 13 or 15d of the 34 Act; or the annual statement of an insurance company not subject to Section 12(g) of the 34 Act; together with any other reports required to be filed at regular intervals under such provisions of the 34 Act which have been filed by the issuer after such annual report or annual statement; or

☐ D. The security of the issuer on which you are submitting a quotation has been the subject of both bid and asked quotations in an interdealer quotation system at specified prices on each of at least 12 days within the previous 30 calendar days with no more than four business days in succession without such a two-way quotation; or

(OVER)

The Harborside Financial Center 600 Plaza Three Jersey City, NJ 07311 (201) 435-9000

NQB FORM 211

FIGURE 1–2. Listing Application for the National Quotation Bureau, Inc. (cont'd.).

☐ E. The security of the issuer of which you are submitting a quotation is admitted to trading on a national securities exchange (as registered under the 34 Act) and has been traded on such an exchange on the same day as, or on the business day next preceding, the day the quotation is published or submitted; or

☐ F. The security of the issuer of which you are submitting a quotation is a security of a foreign issuer exempt from Section 12(g) of the 34 Act by reason of compliance with the provisions of Rule 12(g) 3-2(b) thereunder.

☐ G. None of the above.

If you have checked A or B above, supply a copy of the prospectus or offering circular to National Quotation Bureau with this Form 211.

If your answer was "G. None of the above", please supply the information specified in Part 3.

PART 3

A. Describe the nature of products or services offered by the issuer.

B. Describe the nature and the extent of the issuer's facilities.

C. Indicate the name of the Chief Executive officer and members of the Board of Directors of the issuer.

D. Attach a copy of the issuer's most recent balance sheet and profit and loss retained earning statement.

E. Attach similar financial information for such part of the two preceding fiscal years as the issuer or its predecessor has been in existence.

F. State whether the undersigned, or any person associated with the undersigned, is affiliated directly or indirectly with the issuer.

G. State whether the quotation is being published or submitted on behalf of any other broker-dealer. If so, state the name of such broker or dealer.

H. State whether the quotation is being submitted or published directly or indirectly on behalf of the issuer or any director, officer or any person, directly or indirectly, the beneficial owner of more than 10% of the outstanding units or shares of any equity security of the issuer. If so, state the name of such person and the basis for any exemption under the Federal securities laws for any sales of such securities on behalf of such person.

____

Broker-Dealer Firm Must Be A NQB Subscriber

I certify that I have examined this form and, to the best of my knowledge and belief, it is true, correct and complete. I authorize the National Quotation Bureau, Incorporated to furnish a copy of this questionnaire and any or all of the information contained in this form to the Securities and Exchange Commission or any other regulatory agency.

Name of Broker-Dealer employee to contact regarding information contained herein____________________________ **Phone**__________

Name and Signature of Broker-Dealer Partner or Officer________________________________

Firm Name ________________________________ **Date**__/__/__
(NQB SUBSCRIBER)

Address____________________________________ **Zip**________ considers market making activities just as one of a number of profit centers it operates in. Falling into this second category of market maker would be almost all of the "household name" brokerage firms such as Merrill Lynch and Smith Barney. Frequently you find that wholesale market makers as well as retail market makers make markets in the same stocks. The characters, reputations, and asset bases of the market makers in a particular stock may rightfully influence your decision as to whether or not to invest in the particular stock; however, the kind of market makers—whether wholesale or retail—should not by itself influence your decision (*see* Chapter 2).

As to how much capital a firm is required to have to act in a market-making capacity, the regulatory bodies set down specific requirements. The particular dollar amount of capital required is tied to the number of stocks the broker/dealer makes a market in. If a brokerage firm suffers a loss of capital, the regulatory bodies may require it to curtail its market-making activities.

This discussion of the types of market makers and their capital bases is intended to familiarize you with some of the differences among market makers. These differences are important as you evaluate the "quality" of the market makers you expect to be dealing with (*see* Chapter 2).

The Broker as Agent or Principal

When you, as an investor, instruct your broker to purchase or sell an over-the-counter security, the broker will act either as principal in the transaction or, most commonly, as agent for the customer. The broker who acts *as agent* receives the customer's instruction, and directs the trading desk of the firm employing him or her to go out into the market to purchase or sell the particular security. The trader then identifies those broker/dealers making a market in the stock via the pink sheets or NASDAQ and executes the transaction as directed. The customer is charged a commission for this service.

The other scenario occurs when a brokerage firm acts as principal. Again assume that a customer instructs a broker to purchase or sell a particular over-the-counter security. But in this case assume that the order involves a stock the firm makes a market in. In this case, the broker acts *as principal,* simply buying or selling the stock at the bid or asked price. The customer is not charged a commission on the transaction because the brokerage firm makes its profit from the spread—the difference between the bid and asked price.

Whether a particular broker/dealer acts as principal or agent is of particular significance when you consider purchasing or selling a substantial amount of a particular stock. With large orders, you gain an advantage by placing the order with a brokerage firm that makes a market in the stock. Because the broker can act as principal in the transaction, you, the customer, are able to sell or buy at the bid or asked price net of any commission.

In addition to the savings in commission, a buyer or seller of size gains other advantages by putting the transaction through a market maker. As a market maker, the brokerage firm would be more familiar with the company's present and future prospects and better able to keep the investor informed. Also, in the case of inactively traded over-the-counter stocks (a fertile investment field explored in Chapter 3) market makers may be the only sources of stock.

The description of market makers and OTC transactions presented thus far, while not exhaustive, should be sufficient to give you a brief overview of how the marketplace works. Precise information about the practices of the OTC market including among other things the execution of retail trades, the receipt and delivery of securities, and the Rules of Fair Practice is included in Appendix II, "The Functioning of the NASD," and you are encouraged to familiarize yourself with that material. Now let's go on to discuss some of the relevant features of the OTC market in relation to the exchanges.

NEGOTIATED VS. AUCTION MARKETPLACE

Unlike the OTC market, where transactions are negotiated, the stock exchanges operate as auction marketplaces. A transaction is executed, not by phone between the investor's broker and a market maker, but by the *floor brokers,* also called *commission brokers,* who are physically present on the exchange floor.

On the NYSE, the floor brokers are the individuals who actually execute the buy and sell orders given to the firms employing them. The floor brokers represent the largest group of persons actually making transactions on the floor of the Exchange. A typical trade on the NYSE might be carried out as follows:

John Investor, a customer of Merrill Lynch, decides to sell his holdings in General Motors. The order is entered by the registered representative handling the account and "flashed" to the floor of the Exchange. One of the clerks employed by Merrill Lynch at the Exchange signals one of Merrill Lynch's available floor brokers—say, Bob Broker—that an order has come in to be executed. Once Bob Broker has the order, he proceeds to *the crowd,* that is, to the area where the floor brokers interested in buying or selling General Motors stock are gathered—around the "post" of the specialist in General Motors. (The role of the specialist is discussed in greater detail later; at this point it is sufficient to understand the specialist simply as an "umpire" seeking to maintain an orderly market in the stocks assigned him or her by the Exchange.)

Once he enters the "crowd," Bob Broker's job is to find another floor broker who, acting on the instructions of a customer wishing to buy General Motors stock, can agree to John Investor's terms, that is, to the price and number of shares. He does this by public outcry—by calling out the terms of the order—as is done at auction; thus the term *auction marketplace.*

This brief description highlights the distinction between an auction marketplace (an exchange) and a negotiated marketplace (OTC). In the case of the exchange, once the floor broker enters "the crowd," the whole trading process is subject to public scrutiny. The representatives of the buyer and seller meet face to face. In addition, all transactions involving exchange members are reported on the combined tape so that this information is available to any interested party.

Because the Exchange's trading process is more visible, it may at first glance seem fairer or more equitable than that of the over-the-counter market, but such a conclusion is not really valid. The absence of public outcry and face-to-face contact in the OTC market does not place the buyer or seller at a disadvantage. For one thing, the federal regulatory authorities and the National Association of Securities Dealers, Inc. (NASD) oversee the OTC market and have imposed the same types of rules and regulations that govern trading practices on the exchanges. Thus, the over-the-counter market is as efficient, fair, and equitable as the listed market. This fact, coupled with the ever-increasing movement toward automated trading for over-the-counter stocks, results in a fair, equitable, and liquid marketplace.

SPECIALIST VS. MARKET MAKER

Specialists on the exchange floor have two basic functions: First, they are charged with maintaining fair and orderly markets for the stocks assigned them by the Exchange, that is, they must be prepared to buy stock when the market is declining and to sell stock when it is rising. Specialists are required to have adequate capital to perform this function.

Second, each specialist is given the responsibility for "maintaining the book" in the particular stocks he or she is assigned to make a market in. *Maintaining the book* simply means recording in a "book"—in today's world, a computer terminal—all orders given to him or her for execution by floor brokers. Typically, specialists are given orders that are *away from the market* (that is, at prices above or below the prevailing market). Limit and stop orders (orders calling for the purchase or sale of stock at specific prices) are the kinds of orders left to specialists for execution. The specialist also handles the execution of all odd-lot orders, that is, orders of less than 100 shares.

Because specialists maintain these books, they have a distinct advantage over other investors. By virtue of their position, they know how much demand and supply exists at various prices for the particular stocks they make markets in. They need this information to know what prices to bid and ask for in their market-making role. Because this position is so significant, the activities of specialists are closely monitored by exchange officials. Each specialist's performance is reviewed periodically by the exchange according to certain prescribed statistical guidelines and in the rare instances when abuses are uncovered, disciplinary action is taken.

In a broad sense, the role of the OTC market makers approximates that of the specialists at the NYSE. However, unlike the specialist, whose responsibilities are broadly defined as "maintaining an orderly market," a market maker has only one primary obligation to members of the investing public: to buy or sell 100 shares of the particular stock it makes a market in at its bid or asked price. In industry jargon, it is said that a market maker is held to no more than 100 shares on either side of the market when dealing with a particular customer.

This factor does account, in part, for greater volatility in the OTC market and requires you, as an investor, to be more aware of the reputations, characters, and capital bases of the broker/dealers who make a market in any stock you invest in.

From this section of the book, you can see that there are marked differences in the way listed versus over-the-counter securities trade. Unfortunately, many investors are deterred from investing OTC because of these differences. To put the differences in perspective, let's examine some of the most common objections to the OTC market.

MYTH #1:

The large, well-capitalized, household-name companies are found only among listed stocks.

If you are like most investors, your first investment was probably in a "name" stock. Companies such as AT&T, General Motors, or Dupont—to name just a few of the thousands of listed stocks—are the kinds of companies beginning investors are often most comfortable with because they use those companies' products or services daily. For beginning investors, the fact that many such companies are listed for trading on the major exchanges may lend substance and value to the companies themselves. Also. these "name" stocks are the kinds of investments many registered representatives frequently recommend to their customers.

Despite the commonly held perception that most big companies list their stocks on the exchange, you, as an investor, should be aware that companies such as American Express and Anheuser Busch traded over the counter for decades and became listed only in recent years. To this day, the stocks of most of the nation's banks and insurance companies, as well as a significant number of the country's major industrial and service companies, trade over the counter.

MYTH #2:

Listed stocks represent the only category of truly liquid stocks.

A major concern of many investors new to the over-the-counter marketplace is whether the market is liquid. Liquidity refers to the relative ease or difficulty in buying and selling stocks. Those who argue that the OTC market is illiquid point to the specialist system that supposedly ensures a more liquid marketplace. But depending on which stocks you invest in, the over-the-counter marketplace can be as liquid as the listed market. Liquidity in the over-the-counter market ranges the gamut from extremely liquid in the case of well-capitalized, actively traded stocks to extremely illiquid in the case of small closely held companies. This broad range reflects investor interest and, hence, the number of market makers in a particular stock, rather than the absence of a specialist system.

The wide variations in liquidity necessitate your coming to grips with your attitudes toward investing, the time frames you are willing to hold positions for, and the amount of capital you want to commit to a particular stock. If you are unwilling or unable to live with a high degree of risk even in the face of potentially high rewards, you should probably limit your investments to the large, well-capitalized companies traded over the counter. On the other hand, if you are willing to assume a fair amount of risk, you may decide to invest in a particular stock even though it is relatively illiquid because its selling price is low compared to the value of the company's underlying assets.

The important point is that you must determine in each case how liquid the particular stock is *before* you invest. Chapter 2 describes some general considerations related to liquidity, such as a stock's float and spread. Chapters 3 and 4 present a detailed discussion of liquidity as a characteristic of particular categories of stocks. This information can enable you to assess accurately the liquidity of OTC stocks and avoid the pitfalls that worry many potential OTC investors.

Another important consideration in evaluating the liquidity of the OTC marketplace is the introduction of automated trading. Within the past few years the NASDAQ system for trading over-the-counter stocks has markedly improved the liquidity in this marketplace. Its basic aim is to expedite the trading of over-the-counter stocks. Only the introduction of NASDAQ made it possible for institutions to enter the OTC market to any degree or for individual investors to get rapid execution on OTC trades. The presence of institutional investors in the OTC marketplace confirms that NASDAQ does work.

Likewise, the creation of NASDAQ has revolutionized the way in which OTC stocks are traded and increased investor confidence in the whole marketplace. Although the major market break on October 19, 1987 demonstrated certain weaknesses in the system, the problems would have been far more severe had NASDAQ not been in operation.

MYTH #3:
Information about OTC stocks is hard to obtain.

The availability of information is a major concern of all investors and, in particular, to investors in the over-the-counter market. Lack of information about OTC stocks is a major reason given by many investors for confining their investments to listed securities. But a substantial amount of information is available on OTC stocks if you know where and how to get it.

Table 1–1 presents the major sources of information on OTC stocks together with a description of the kind of information you can extract from each. Note that most of these sources can be used in connection with listed as well as OTC stocks.

The listing should help you realize that the sources of information about over-the-counter stocks fall into two general categories—written and numerical. But another source of information often overlooked is the management of the companies whose OTC-traded stocks you are considering investing in. Specific information about how to use the written sources and how to approach and evaluate a company's management is provided in Chapter 5.

A final note about market information that should be mentioned in connection with a NASDAQ listing is that NASDAQ releases daily to the media two listings of OTC stocks. One list, referred to as the National List, includes most of the more actively traded, nationally known OTC stocks. The other, known as the Additional List, includes relatively less active stocks that are regional in nature and generally lower priced. This daily listing of NASDAQ stocks enables you, as an investor, to monitor your OTC NASDAQ stocks on a daily basis as easily as you can monitor listed stocks. Monitoring OTC stocks that are not NASDAQ listed is no more difficult than a phone call to your broker.

MYTH #4:

The OTC market is not as "safe" as the listed market.

Concerns about the manner in which business is conducted in the over-the-counter market also leads investors (both novice and sophisticated) to shun that marketplace. But as discussed in connection with the concept of a negotiated vs. an auction market, the rules of the game in the over-the-counter market are on their face as fair and equitable as those governing trading in listed stocks. Of course, just as individuals occasionally abuse their positions in connection with transactions in listed stocks, people sometimes abuse their

TABLE 1–1. Sources of Information About OTC Stocks.

Source	*Type of Information Provided*
SEC filings (10K, 10Q, proxy, annual report, and the like)	Most complete presentation of information (both textual and numerical) on publicly traded companies
Standard & Poor's, Moody's, and relevant databases	Material drawn from SEC filings in a more readable format
Wall Street Journal, Barrons, and other financial newspapers	Provide up-to-date information on corporate and economic developments
Wall Street Transcript	Contains research reports on publicly traded companies, both listed and unlisted, submitted by brokerage firms
Spectrum	Quarterly listing of the stocks owned and positions added to by virtually all investment companies, advisors, and limited partnerships
The Unlisted Market Guide	Provides information on OTC stocks similar to that presented in the S&P Stock Guide with particular emphasis on those not closely followed by the investment community
Wall Street Journal Index, Funk & Scott Index, Lexus, and other databases	Alphabetical directory of newspaper and magazine articles on publicly traded companies, both listed and unlisted
Association of Individual Investors and its publications	An association of individuals whose avocation is investing. The organization provides a wealth of information and material on many companies not followed by investment professionals (that is, shadow stocks)
Newsletters, magazines, and advisory services	Of varying usefulness. Appendix I provides a detailed list of such services

positions in the OTC marketplace by taking unfair advantage of the investing public.

What is the day-to-day practice in the OTC market and how are the rules of the game enforced? Because these questions are so important and because practices are changing, Appendix II of this book is devoted to describing the work of the self-regulatory body governing the over-the-counter market. In addition, Appendix IV discusses the grievance procedures available to you if you feel you have been defrauded. At this point, however, it would be appropriate to familiarize you with the approach taken toward governing OTC stock trading and thus dispel some of the fears about participating in that marketplace that many investors express.

As with listed stocks, not until after the Crash of 1929 and the advent of the New Deal were rules and regulations imposed on the OTC marketplace and its participants. The Maloney Act, enacted in 1938 as an amendment to the Securities Exchange Act of 1934, provided the legal means by which brokerage firms not subject to stock exchange rules and regulations could offer investors an equal degree of ethical and proprietary responsibility in securities transactions.[1] This movement toward fairness and equality in OTC dealings has expanded and grown over the years.

The NASD is the hub of the regulatory apparatus governing the trading of over-the-counter stocks. Effectively, all broker/dealer organizations registered with the U.S. Securities & Exchange Commission in the United States are members of the NASD and consequently are governed by its rules and regulations. The fundamental philosophy of the NASD is best expressed in these words from its bylaws: "... a member in the conduct of his business, shall observe high standards of commercial honor and just and equitable principles of trade."

Just what rules does the NASD enforce? The bylaws, as the rules are called, are divided into four distinct categories: The Uniform Practice Code defines the way member firms

[1]Pessin, Allan H., *The Illustrated Encyclopedia of the Securities Industry*, New York Institute of Finance, NY, 1988, p. 235.

must deal with each other; the Code of Procedure spells out the procedures to be followed in the case of violations and complaints; the Rules of Fair Practice describe how a member firm must conduct itself when dealing with members of the investing public; and the Code of Arbitration spells out procedures for arbitrating disputes between brokerage firms and public customers.

The key provisions of the bylaws are listed and described in Appendix II, so it is not necessary to repeat them here. But to give you an idea of how the NASD works to make the over-the-counter marketplace a safe place to invest your money, we present here a typical example of an NASD rule: the 5% markup policy.

This rule, which is part of the Rules of Fair Practice, requires brokerage firms to sell stock to the investing public at prices that are "fair and reasonable" in relation to prevailing market conditions. The NASD felt that under normal market conditions a broker acting as principal in a transaction should earn no more than 5% profit on a transaction with a customer. Because many factors can influence what is fair and reasonable, the 5% markup policy represents a guideline, not a hard-and-fast rule. However, brokerage firms must be prepared to defend themselves against complaints by customers about unreasonable markups. If a firm is found to be in violation of the "fair and reasonable" standard, disciplinary action is taken by the NASD. This example should help you see that the regulation of the OTC market by the NASD enables you to expect equitable trade practices and provides the opportunity for you to gain satisfaction if you feel you have been taken advantage of. In these respects, the OTC market is as "safe" as the listed market.

Having finished this chapter, you should have a basic understanding of the OTC marketplace: how transactions are made, how the market-maker system works, and what the basic jargon means. Hopefully you have also achieved some level of comfort with the idea of investing over the counter and have realized that the most common objections to the OTC marketplace need not present obstacles to the knowledgeable investor. The following chapters are intended to give you the information you need to invest over the counter intelligently and profitably.

2

Getting the Most from Your OTC Investments

To make the most of your ventures into the OTC market, you need to be aware of that market's peculiarities. The foregoing chapter discussed some common objections to investing in the OTC marketplace and showed you that those objections need not discourage you from taking advantage of the excellent opportunities available there. On the other hand, an awareness of the differences between trading on an exchange and trading OTC should help you to beware of possible pitfalls. This chapter presents some general guidelines and strategies we call "Trading Rules" to help you make the most of your OTC investments.

TRADING RULE ONE: KNOW YOURSELF

"Whatever investment arena you choose, the first imperative is to know yourself. Evaluating your assets and liabilities is the first task. The investment techniques and stocks you choose must be appropriate for your aims and goals."

The majority of individuals who are active in the financial marketplace think of themselves as investors rather than traders. "Investing" has a certain aura of respectability whereas "trading" conjures up images of gambling and scenes from Las Vegas and Atlantic City. In reality, the successful investor must be part trader and the successful trader should possess some traits of an investor.

Before you can apply the trading rules described in this chapter, you should explore the question of whether you are characteristically an investor or a trader. One major difference is represented by the number of transactions you enter into over the span of a year. A typical investor may have ten or fewer transactions in a given year; a typical trader may have fifty or more transactions in the same time period. How much time you devote to managing your investments also tends to characterize you as an investor or a trader. Investors typically check the prices of their stocks no more than daily; traders may telephone their brokers as many as four or five times a day. Investors may hold a stock for decades; traders, on the other hand, may invest in ten or twenty different stocks during the course of a single year.

The types of stocks you choose can also distinguish you as primarily an investor or a trader. For many people, listed stocks represent investment quality, while over-the-counter issues are considered the domain of traders. In Chapter 1 this idea was shown to be a myth, but it is true that certain types of OTC stocks such as penny stocks and the stocks of bankrupt companies are better suited to traders. These stocks often carry high risk/reward ratios. On the other hand, blue chip stocks, banks and insurance companies, and regional smokestack company stocks are generally considered the domain of investors. (Chapters 3 and 4 describe these categories in some detail along with specific information about evaluating individual stocks.)

Your investment philosophy probably includes elements of both investing and trading. If you are like most people, the number of transactions you make and your level of interest fluctuate during your lifetime. Likewise, you will probably not confine yourself to investing exclusively in one category or type of stock. To be successful, you need to combine the elements of an investor ("number crunching") with the elements of a trader (a "feel" for the market).

The important point here is that, whatever your investment philosophy, *you* must decide how much risk you are willing to accept and live with in light of the level of return you hope for. The risk/reward ratio is the cornerstone of any investment decision or selection process. Your investment aims and goals, along with a realistic appraisal of your risk tolerance, determine the risk/reward ratio that is appropriate for you. With these figures in mind the other parts of the process will fall into place.

TRADING RULE TWO: SELECT YOUR BROKER CAREFULLY

> "When investing in OTC stocks it is crucial that you locate a brokerage firm active in that marketplace. Likewise, it is essential that you establish a relationship with a particular registered representative who is both familiar with the OTC marketplace and with whom you share a common approach to investing or trading."

The selection of the brokerage firm you use and, in particular, the registered representative who actually handles your account is a crucial factor in determining your success or failure in the OTC marketplace. Unfortunately, in most instances, the brokerage firm or the particular registered representative is the one who solicits the investor's business rather than the other way around. For best results, you should make an active search for and a conscious selection of the firm and registered rep.

Use the same approach in selecting a brokerage firm and registered rep as you would use in selecting a family lawyer, doctor, or accountant. The best source for potential candidates is probably the personal recommendation of family and friends. The second best source of potential candidates is through your own personal search via financial publications, investment advisory services, and related areas for names of potential brokers. Once you have identified potential candidates, you are ready to undertake the second step of this two-stage process: interviewing the firm and the particular registered rep you are thinking of using. From this interview, you want to learn not just the charges for executing trades or the stocks the firm makes a market in—although these considerations are relevant—but, more important, you want to find out whether the particular firm's and registered representative's approach to investing fits your own. If you are an aggressive trader willing to accept large losses in return for the possibility of large gains, an aggressive brokerage firm or registered rep may be the one for you. However, if your orientation is toward the preservation of capital and if you are unwilling or unable to assume large risks comfortably, such a brokerage firm or registered rep would not suit you. The key point is to be honest with yourself and to come to terms with the broker. Discuss your investment goals and aims clearly and bluntly with the registered rep who will eventually handle your trades in over-the-counter stocks.

In addition to a compatible investment philosophy, you want to know that your brokerage firm and registered representative have ideas and concepts to offer you. You don't need a registered rep who works from a script, that is, who has no independent ideas. Although brokerage is first and foremost a commission business, any registered representative you select should be capable of independent thought and should not merely work from a list of recommended stocks the brokerage firm puts together.

Follow-through and long-range planning are two other traits to look for in the brokerage firm and registered rep you select. Be sure the brokerage firm and its employees have staying power—that both will be available for advice and counsel after you have given them an order and they have earned their commission. In the same vein, the brokerage firm and registered rep you select should think beyond simply recommending particular transactions and should come up with some long-range plans for making your assets grow over the next two to five years.

At this point it might be appropriate to alert the reader to the potential dangers of dealing with cold callers. Cold callers are registered representatives who call individuals on a random basis trying to interest them either in opening accounts with their firms or in specific investment ideas. While cold calling is a common way for registered representatives to obtain new accounts and customers, you should ask some very specific and pointed questions before you decide to do business with a registered rep whom you know only as a voice over the telephone. If you are unable to get answers to basic questions such as how long the brokerage firm has been in business or what information you can obtain about the financials of the particular stock the rep is recommending, or if a cold caller promises you a "guaranteed profit on your investment"—don't do business with that individual.

Another question that may come to mind when you consider selecting a broker is what role a discount broker should play in your OTC investment program. The answer to this questions depends on you, the individual investor. If you are interested in doing your own research, if you come up with your own investment ideas and identify particular stocks worth investing in, and if you have some familiarity with the way OTC stocks are traded, it might be appropriate for you to use the services of a discount broker. If you are such a sophisticated investor you may be simply looking for an order taker to execute the transactions you have already decided on. On the other hand, if you do not have either the time or the inclination to come up with your own investment ideas, a discount broker will not meet your needs; you would be better served by a full-service broker responsible for coming up with investment ideas and for assuming overall responsibility for the management of your account.

If you are already using a particular brokerage firm and registered representative to handle your over-the-counter transactions, certain danger signals may warn you that the brokerage firm and/or registered rep are not right for you. If your broker constantly suggests you switch from one to another of the stocks the firm makes a market in or discourages you from selling a particular stock he or she has put you into or refuses to execute your specific sell order, you should consider moving your account to another brokerage firm. A registered rep who is frequently unavailable to you and does not return your telephone calls promptly is also flashing you a danger signal, which should alert you to switch brokers. Common sense dictates that you do business only with a broker you have faith in and who provides dependable service as well as profitable investment ideas.

TRADING RULE THREE: KNOW THE MARKET MAKERS

> "Market makers play a crucial role in how a particular over-the-counter stock is traded. Before investing in any OTC stock, learn about the broker/dealers who make a market in that stock. The number of market makers, the quality of the market makers, the appearance of new market makers or the absence of old ones, and whether the stock is listed on NASDAQ have a bearing on your approach to trading the stock."

How Many Market Makers?

Obviously, stocks with only a few market makers are less liquid—that is, more difficult to buy and sell—than those with many. Acquiring a substantial number of shares without driving up the stock's price or selling a large block without unduly depressing the price is difficult. If you purchase a stock with three or fewer market makers, you should be prepared to hold a position for a long time. Regional smokestack companies and some blue chip stocks are examples of types of stocks with limited numbers of market makers.

Is It NASDAQ Listed?

A NASDAQ listing makes it easy to monitor the particular OTC stock: A vast amount of information is as close as the nearest terminal. In addition, NASDAQ-listed stocks are generally more liquid than non-NASDAQ-listed stocks. Perhaps of greatest significance is the fact that a NASDAQ listing carries with it the ability to margin the particular stock. So you can see that a NASDAQ listing makes it much easier for you to invest or trade in the particular OTC stock. Blue chips, banks and insurance companies, and international companies represent the principal categories of over-the-counter stocks with NASDAQ listings.

What About Market Maker Turnover?

Exploring the significance of any change in the make-up of the group of broker/dealers acting as market makers in a particular stock can give you some important clues about what may be happening with the stock. For example, the appearance of a stock-exchange member firm as a market maker in a stock that was previously the exclusive domain of OTC brokers might signal institutional interest in the stock. Likewise, the appearance in the sheets of a major wholesale market maker could mean that the stock has been discovered by substantial investors. On the other hand, if long-term market makers drop out of a stock, that action may signal that investors have lost interest in the company.

How Good Are the Market Makers?

This factor is perhaps the most difficult-to-define aspect of market makers. Quality includes everything from the net capital of the market-making firm to such intangibles as a market maker's reputation or character. Information as to a market maker's net capital is readily available from the brokerage firm itself or from filings with the SEC, but for the most part you can gain information about a particular market maker's reputation only from personal experience or from conversations with other investors.

As you become more experienced dealing in the OTC marketplace, you will learn that marginal firms can be found among wholesale market makers as well as retail firms, and the only clues to identifying a marginal firm is its lack of capital, high-pressure sale techniques, or reputation.

Before we go on to discuss how the quality of market makers affects a stock's price, one last observation may be relevant: Just as there are good and bad specialists on the floor of an exchange, there are good and bad market makers. Simply put, a "bad" market maker does not seek to service the investing public by maintaining as narrow a spread as the marketplace permits between the bid and asked prices of the stocks it makes a market in. A "good" market maker tries to maintain an orderly market for the stocks it trades. For example, a "good" market maker will not drop a stock by a point or two on a hundred-share trade but instead will seek to moderate price changes. You will not need to be active in the OTC market for long before you learn to distinguish between good and bad market makers. At times you may decide not to invest in a particular OTC stock simply because of the firms that make a market in the stock.

How Does the Quality of the Market Makers Affect a Stock's Price?

Market makers tend to trade in *quality levels*—that is, high-quality market makers such as stock-exchange member firms and wholesale market makers tend to trade in the same stocks whereas low-quality market makers such as thinly capitalized firms and underwriters tend to trade in their own specific stocks. Therefore, you are unlikely to find a wholesale market maker trading in the same stock as a highly leveraged new-issue firm. Such a "class" factor has a real impact on the stock in terms of both investor perception and price volatility. For example, if the market makers in a particular stock were considered marginal, many investors—both individual and professional—would view the stock as highly speculative and not invest in it at all. Such a stock would be characterized as a "traders' stock" and consequently would be likely to assume the characteristic of such a stock, that is, a high degree of price volatility.

New issues of stock are probably impacted by this quality factor to the greatest degree. This is true simply because, as a new issue, a stock has no track record and investors' perceptions of it are largely based on their perceptions of the brokerage firm that took the company public. As an individual investor you can turn this to your advantage by scanning the new issues to identify those that have assets and earnings but are neglected simply on the basis of their parentage—that is, because they have been underwritten by a marginal brokerage firm.

TRADING RULE FOUR: UNDERSTAND THE SIGNIFICANCE OF THE STOCK'S FLOAT

> "The *float* of a particular over-the-counter stock, that is, the number of shares available in the marketplace, helps determine what approach you should take when investing or trading in the stock. Because a stock's float influences who makes a market in the stock, who invests or trades in the stock, and the stock's price volatility, you should calculate the float and understand its influence on the stock before you make an investment."

What Is Float?

Float is an important concept for anyone interested in investing or trading in over-the-counter stocks. Because the OTC market is a negotiated marketplace without listing requirements (that is, minimum requirements for asset base, earnings, and number of shares outstanding) the concept of float has singular relevance for OTC trading.

Just what is meant by the term float? The *float* of a stock refers to the number of shares available in the marketplace.

To calculate a stock's float, subtract from the number of shares outstanding the number of shares owned by insiders (that is, officers, directors, and shareholders of 5% or more); institutions (that is, mutual funds, bank trust departments, insurance companies, and the like); and shares held in the company's treasury. Standard & Poor's Stock Guide provides information about the number of institutional owners and the number of shares they own. A company's Proxy Statement furnishes the number of shares owned by insiders, and the company's Balance Sheet indicates the number of shares held in the company's treasury.

The following step-by-step example shows how to calculate a stock's float.

The Float of XYZ's Common Stock

The number of shares outstanding	9,000,000
The number of shares owned by insiders	–3,000,000
The number of shares owned by institutions	–3,000,000
The float (number of freely trading shares)	3,000,000

How Does Float Affect a Stock?

A stock with a small float, (that is, 5 million shares or less) is generally more volatile than a stock with a sizable float, simply because the small float stock lacks the depth and liquidity to absorb a sizable purchase or sale. For the most part, institutional investors require that a stock have liquidity, which is another way of saying that a stock should have a sufficient float to enable an institutional investor to acquire or dispose of a substantial number of shares without unduly raising or lowering the stock's price. Most institutional investors would invest only in stocks whose floats are 5 million shares or more. For that matter, most individual investors hesitate to invest in stocks with extremely small floats. You can see that float influences who invests in the particular stock. In addition, the size of the float largely determines which brokerage firms make a market in the stock. Stocks with thin floats typically attract the attention of only a select group of market makers who specialize in such stocks, whereas actively traded stocks with sizable floats attract the attention of more and diverse types of market makers.

How Does Float Affect Your Investment?

If you were to invest in a stock with a sizable float, you would be able to liquidate the position easily. The competition between market makers would keep the spread (the difference between bid and asked prices) small. With such a stock, you need not be committed to holding the shares for a long time and you can be somewhat less concerned about buying at the "right" price.

Conversely, you may find yourself "married" to a stock with a thin float for the simple reason that the substantial spread would necessitate your taking a sizable loss to sell out the stock shortly after acquiring it. Also, thinly traded stocks demand that you shop around to obtain the best price since the number of market makers is fewer and hence the competition is less.

TRADING RULE FIVE: CONSIDER THE SPREAD BETWEEN BID AND ASKED PRICES

> "The *spread* between a particular stock's bid price (the price market makers are willing to pay for it) and its asked price (the price market makers are willing to sell it for) bears on whether and how you trade or invest in that stock. A narrow spread indicates that shares can be bought or sold relatively easily; a wide spread suggests that selling a large number of shares quickly and profitably may be difficult. Understanding the factors that influence spread patterns and the typical patterns for the different types of OTC stocks is essential in selecting a stock and in planning your strategy for managing an investment."

What Factors Determine the Spread?

A large float (that is, a large number of shares in public hands) generally narrows the spread between bid and asked prices. Stocks with large floats generally have many market makers; hence, the competition is intense and bid and asked prices are close. Stocks traded via NASDAQ typically have narrow spreads between bid and asked prices.

The type of stock also influences the spread. As a general rule, lower-priced stocks and regional smokestack company stocks have wider spreads between their bid and asked prices. Many bankrupt stocks, penny stocks, low-priced new issues, and regional stocks routinely trade with spreads substantially more than the 5% guideline prescribed by NASD regulations. Some thinly traded regional stocks may have spreads of 30% or more. On the other hand, typically blue chips, international stocks traded over the counter, and banks and insurance companies generally display narrow spreads between bid and asked prices—5 to 15%—although even these categories have exceptions to the rule.

How Should the Spread Influence Your Approach?

If a stock has a narrow spread, you can assume that the market makers are aware of the competition surrounding the stock; therefore you can be less concerned with shopping around for the best price. In addition, a narrow spread between bid and asked prices generally indicates that the stock is attractive to both individual and professional traders because the narrow spread makes it easier to accumulate and dispose of large blocks of stock. Many institutional investors favor OTC stocks having a narrow spread.

Institutional interest—that is, ownership of 20% or more of a company's common stock—typically means that the stock has been discovered by market professionals. As such, the particular stock no longer represents a "bargain" and will be subject to more volatile price swings as it is bought and sold by various institutional investors.

The intention here is not to suggest that you should trade or invest only in OTC stocks with narrow spreads. You should be aware, however, that trading/investing in stocks with wide spreads requires more in the way of knowledge and experience. Before you invest in a stock with a wide spread between bid and asked prices determine whether the anticipated returns are sufficient to warrant the liquidity you are sacrificing and be sure you are willing to make a possible long-term investment, since a wide spread may make it difficult and costly to liquidate the position.

An Alternative

One way of building up a position in a stock that is thinly traded and has a wide spread is to have the brokerage firm you use go into the pink sheets and bid for stock for you. If you feel that a stock offers potentially high returns, this course of action might be appropriate for you because it would reduce the average price you would pay for the stock. In fact, this approach might be the only way to acquire a meaningful position in the stock.

TRADING RULE SIX: DECIDE WHETHER MARGIN TRADING IS APPROPRIATE

> "Leverage is a vital tool that can be used to significant advantage. Before you trade or invest in over-the-counter stocks, determine whether trading on margin is right for you as an individual, familiarize yourself with the rules governing margin trading, and understand how the use of margin relates to the particular trade."

Whether you as an investor decide to utilize margin depends to a large measure on your particular financial situation, your attitude toward debt, and your projections about an investment's return—both in terms of a percentage figure and a time period. Leverage (margin) is a two-edged sword: It can serve to magnify losses as well as gains.

In connection with deciding whether to execute a purchase in a cash or a margin account, you should realize that securities purchased on margin are held by the brokerage firm you are doing business with and remain under control of that firm. The amount of money you must deposit with the broker to finance the transaction is spelled out in the Regulation T requirements for initial margin, administered by the Federal Reserve Board. In the recent past, initial margin requirements have ranged from a high of 75% to the current rate of 50%. At a 50% initial requirement you must put up 50 cents in cash for every 1 dollar of securities purchased.

If you buy stock on margin and its price falls, you may receive a *margin call,* that is, you may be called on to put up additional cash to securities to maintain your position with the stock. The amount you must deposit with the broker to maintain your stock position if the price falls is referred to as *maintenance margin*. In the case of OTC stocks the maintenance margin requirements are administered by the NASD. The important point for you to realize is that whenever you purchase stock on margin and plan to maintain the position, you need to have assets in reserve to meet a margin call if one is made.

In addition, you should be aware that not all OTC stocks are marginable. Only those whose names appear on the OTC Margin List published by the Federal Reserve Board are eligible to be purchased on margin. In order for a stock to appear on this list, a company must meet certain standards regarding assets, earnings, and number of shareholders. Most blue chip companies, banks and insurance companies, new issues (not eligible until 30 days after issue), and international companies can be purchased on margin, whereas bankrupt companies penny stocks, and the stocks of most regional companies are not eligible.

When you consider purchasing a nonmarginable stock, be aware that you are limited as to the amount of profit you can realize simply because you have to pay cash for the shares you purchase. Expressed another way, leverage can be an extremely useful tool in that it gives you added buying power and can magnify your return. Forgoing leverage to pay cash for an unmarginable stock can certainly be worthwhile, but be sure you evaluate the anticipated return in light of this potential disadvantage.

TRADING RULE SEVEN: FOR LONG-TERM COMMITMENTS CONSIDER SPREADING OUT YOUR PURCHASES OVER TIME

> "Buying programs and dollar cost averaging are two investment techniques that can help the individual investor even out the ups and downs of the marketplace. By evening out the timing of your investments, program buying helps mitigate the emotional factor and can help you acquire a large position at a better-than-average price. Particularly in the case of long-term commitments, you should consider timing your investments by some mechanical program."

Timing is an important consideration in connection with any form of investing and something you should always consider once you decide to purchase a particular stock. Timing is particularly important for OTC stocks with wide spreads between bid and asked prices and few market makers, since such stocks generally represent long-term commitments.

In a typical scenario, an individual investor buys as many shares of a particular stock as he or she can afford at the time. Unfortunately, in doing so, the investor might conceivably purchase a large block of stock at its yearly high price. A better approach to acquiring a large position is to use a buying program. Rather than purchase as many shares as you can afford at one time, start in a small way, buying as few as 50 shares the first time. The fact that you own the stock will cause you to follow its price movements. Over time, as you become more familiar with the company and the price range in which the stock trades, you develop what market professionals call a "feel" for the stock. At that point, you can add to your position gradually, until you reach the desired number of shares.

This technique represents perhaps the simplest form of buying program. Although it can help you avoid the pitfall of purchasing a large block of stock at a high price, it remains dependent on your "feel" for the stock and hence leaves your purchase decisions subject to your emotions. Other, more mechanical, programs such as dollar cost averaging mitigate this factor as well.

Dollar cost averaging calls for investing a fixed number of dollars in a selected stock at predetermined intervals of time. For example, once you select a particular over-the-counter stock you want to accumulate, you may decide to purchase $2500 worth of stock every three months. If you use a discount brokerage firm the transaction costs should be relatively low. Although this technique enables you to make purchases at an average price rather than at the yearly high or low price and to eliminate emotion from the investment process, it does not guarantee a profit in every instance. Selecting the right stock is still the deciding factor as to whether you make or lose money. Chapters 3 and 4 discuss how to select the right OTC stocks for profitable investing.

3

Choosing Substantial OTC Stocks for Investment

The kinds of stocks traded over the counter range from substantial to marginal—from what could be characterized as blue chips to others that could be described as cats and dogs. The absence of listing requirements (with the exception of the NASDAQ listing requirements) means that every possible category of public company can be found trading over the counter.

This chapter and Chapter 4 describe the principal categories or types of stocks traded over the counter. The majority of over-the-counter stocks fall into one of the following categories:

- blue chips
- new issues (start-up or substantial)
- stocks of banks, savings and loan associations, and insurance companies
- "smokestack America" (regional companies)
- stocks of bankrupt companies
- penny stocks

- stocks of international companies

Knowing which category a stock falls into is important because each type of stock has certain peculiarities. Familiarity with these peculiarities helps you develop an approach or strategy for trading in the stock and can be critical to deciding whether the stock is right for you at all. For example, knowing which category an over-the-counter stock fits into can tell you how easy or difficult it would be to acquire a substantial position in the stock and how easy or difficult it would be to dispose of the position. For example, it is difficult to acquire a large number of shares of many regional, thinly traded smokestack companies, and because the spread between bid and asked prices for such stocks is often substantial, they do not lend themselves to being "traded." In many instances, the investor becomes "married" to such stocks, that is, he or she must hold the stock for a long time.

These two chapters describe the characteristics of particular types of stocks in detail, with emphasis on how to evaluate individual stocks in each category. Chapter 3 describes stocks that might be preferred by "investors," notably blue chip and substantial new issues and the stocks of banks, thrifts, insurance companies, and smokestack industries. Chapter 4 discusses those OTC stocks generally preferred by "traders." It is important to note that, just as the difference between investors and traders is actually one of degree—successful traders have some characteristics of investors and vice versa—the classification of a stock as an investors' stock or a traders' stock is a relative one. Stocks described as investors' stocks tend to have substantial assets, earnings, and capitalization, relatively low risk/reward ratios and/or may be more difficult to trade; the reverse is true of those stocks characterized as traders' stocks. Remember though, that these classifications are broad and general and that, depending on the particular stock itself, either an "investor" or a "trader" can make profitable transactions in stocks of either type.

BLUE CHIP STOCKS

The term *blue chip company* generally refers to a firm with substantial assets, earnings, and capitalization. Figure 3–1 contains a list of OTC companies that might best be described as blue chips.

If the number and variety of blue chips surprises you, it may be because many investors have been indoctrinated with the notion that only the stocks of marginal companies trade over the counter. In reality, many companies with substantial assets, earnings, and capital structures call the OTC marketplace home.

Why are so many blue chips found trading over the counter? In most cases the managements of these companies have found that the OTC marketplace meets their needs in every way. They feel that an exchange listing offers them no particular advantage. This has been especially true in recent years for a number of reasons, not least of which has been the greater access to and liquidity of the over-the-counter market that NASDAQ provides. In addition, the interest of individual investors in the OTC market has grown and even institutional investors have demonstrated greater acceptance of and participation in the OTC market.

Another factor that might play a role in a particular management's decision to keep its stock over the counter is an unwillingness on the part of management to give up control of its stock. Management may fear attracting attention to the company as a potential takeover target. Such concerns can be particularly important in the case of a regional company whose stock is thinly traded and not actively followed by professional investors. Indeed, such a company can represent a real buying opportunity for you as an individual investor.

Characteristics of Blue Chip Stocks

Blue chip stocks, whether traded over the counter or on an exchange, share certain common characteristics. First, because of the size of their assets, earnings, and capitalization,

FIGURE 3–1. Listing of OTC Blue Chips.

A

Aceto Corp.
Amcast Industrial Corp.
Associated Communications Corp.
Aritech Corp.

C

William Carter Co.
Chicago Dock & Canal Trust
Cobe Laboratories, Inc.
Cintas, Inc.

D

Douglas & Lomason, Inc.
Daisy Systems Corp.

F

Forscher Group, Inc.

G

G & K Services, Inc.
Grey Advertising
Genzxyme Corp.

H

Hyponex Corp.

J

Jacobson Stores, Inc.
Jones Intercable, Inc.
Jefferson Smurfit, Inc.

K

Kenan Transport, Inc.

L

Lilly Industrial Coating, Inc.
Arthur D. Little, Inc.
Liqui Box, Inc.
Longview Fiber Co.
Leisure Concepts, Inc.

M

McFarland Energy, Inc.
Mosinee Paper Co.
Marsh Supermarkets, Inc.
Molex, Inc.

N

Neutragena Corp.
J.C. Nichols Corp.

O

Oshkosh B'Gosh Corp.

Q

Quaker Chemical Co.

R

Rule Industries, Inc.
Radionics, Inc.
Rose's Stores, Inc.
Roto-Rooter, Inc.
RPM, Inc.

S

Sanford Corp.
Stryker Corp.
Southern California Water Co.
Sun Microsystems, Inc.
Southwest Water Co.
Standard Commercial Tobacco Co.
Shorewood Packaging Co.

U

Uniforce Temporary Personnel, Inc.
United Stationers, Inc.

V

V-Band, Inc.

W

Western Steer—Mom & Pops, Inc.
Western Publishing, Inc.
Worthington Industries, Inc.
Wiser Oil, Inc.
WD-40, Inc.

they have historically proven to be the safest and least volatile stocks to invest in. Blue chip stocks have traditionally offered the investor less in the way of growth and more in the way of safety. Second, blue chip stocks, whether traded over the counter or listed on an exchange, lend themselves to such investment strategies as dollar cost averaging. And because blue chips typically lead overall market movements (whether up or down), they lend themselves well to systems of purchasing based on the up- or downturns in the economy. Finally, if you are new to the over-the-counter market, you may find it appropriate—at least initially—to invest in the OTC blue chips. As you become more familiar with the way stocks are traded in the OTC marketplace and the variety of stocks found there, you will likely want to expand your portfolio to include stocks selected from one or more of the other categories of OTC stocks.

SUBSTANTIAL NEW ISSUES

In the minds of many investors, the new-issue market is synonymous with the over-the-counter market. New issues account for a high proportion of OTC stocks.

Types of New Issues

The stocks of virtually all public companies are first traded over the counter and only later move to the exchanges. Therefore, new issues may well represent the most diverse category of stock traded over the counter. Some new issues represent companies that are substantial factors in their respective industries, with proven track records in terms of sales and earnings and significant assets in the way of cash, plant, or equipment. Such new issues are typically underwritten by a number of major brokerage firms. Alternatively, a new issue may represent a start-up, concept-type company with little in the way of earnings, assets, or financial backing. Start-up companies, because of their more speculative nature, are discussed in Chapter 4.

In evaluating a new issue, first determine which category—substantial or start-up—the issue represents. You can do this simply by reading the prospectus (you would be surprised how few investors actually do this before investing their money) or by reviewing the company's annual report if the company has been public for a year or more. The prospectus carries on its face a description of the risk factors attached to the offering. A company with a number of risk factors and little in the way of assets by definition represents a start-up operation. A company with strong financials and few risk factors obviously represents a substantial company.

Selecting Substantial New Issues

Once you have drawn your conclusion, you can determine the approach to use in analyzing the company to decide whether to invest in it at all. In the case of a substantial or seasoned company, number crunching can really help you to decide whether the stock is a buy or not. Such a company or new issue has a track record of sales, earnings, and return on equity figures for you to work with. (The numerical techniques and ratios to use in making your analysis are described in detail in Appendix III.)

The recent market break has created a number of "bargains" among substantial companies that have recently gone public. Figure 3–2 lists a number of these substantial new issues. In many instances such stocks have declined in price by 50% or more since October 19, 1987. The suggestion here is not that you simply go out and purchase all of these issues, since they are at such "bargain" prices. Rather, they are listed here to give you now—at perhaps the best time to invest in such issues—the opportunity to apply to them the analytical techniques described in Appendix III.

Scanning the list of recent new issues shows you that such issues have a number of things in common. Many of these initial public offerings (IPOs) represent the opportunity to invest in companies that occupy dominant positions in their particular industry or market niche. Many of these new issues represent regional companies that at the present time are not actively followed by many investment professionals. Also, many of these offerings have a limited number of shares outstanding—typically on the order of two or three million shares—and thus offer the opportunity for potential stock splits and rapid upward price movement once they are rediscovered by institutional investors and the investment community in general.

BANKS, SAVINGS AND LOANS, AND INSURANCE COMPANIES

Banks, savings and loans, and insurance companies represent another important category of stocks traded over the counter—one in which the individual investor is on an equal footing with institutional/professional investors. Until about fifteen years ago virtually all the nation's banks and insurance companies were traded over the counter. Since then, many of the major money-center banks and prominent insurance companies have sought and obtained listings on the major exchanges—most commonly the NYSE. The drive for an exchange listing stemmed largely from a desire on the part of these banks and insurance companies to stimulate institutional interest in their stock. But the vast majority of the country's banks, savings and loans (thrifts), and regional insurance companies still trade over the counter. Because many of these stocks are not largely dominated by institutional and professional investors, they represent buying opportunities for knowledgeable individual investors.

Figure 3–3 lists regional banks, savings and loan associations, and insurance companies traded over the counter. You may find it worthwhile to review this list to see how many you are already familiar with through personal business dealings. Almost invariably individual investors are surprised to learn that their local savings and loans or insurers are indeed publicly traded companies.

Just how do you evaluate banks, thrifts, and insurance companies and choose those that are appropriate for you to invest in? As a starting point, let's discuss some of the

FIGURE 3–2. Listing of Substantial New Issues.

Substantial new issues encompass those companies which have assets and/or earnings at the time of the publication of this book. Further, the following companies have had their initial public offering since 1985. (New and secondary issues.)

A

ACC Corporation, Inc.
Aaron Brothers Art Marts, Inc.
Acceptance Insurance Holding, Inc.
Action Auto Stores, Inc.
Acuson Corp.
Adams Russell Electronics Corp.
Armor All Products Corp.
American Woodmark Corp.
Guy F. Atkinson of California, Inc.

B

Barricini Foods, Inc.
Barrister Information Systems Corp.
Bay Head Ventures, Inc.
Beauty Labs, Inc.
Brandon Systems, Inc.
Bonneville Pacific, Inc.

C

Canonie Environmental Corp.
Cadnetix Corp.
Calgon Carbon Corp.
Cancom International, Inc.
Canton International Corp.
Carolina Mountain Holding Co.
Cellular, Inc.
Clairson International Corp.
Convergent Solutions, Inc.

D

Dairy Mart Convenience Stores, Inc.
Daxor Corp.
Decatur Capital Corp.
Delta Woodside Industries, Inc.

E

Envirosafe Services, Inc.
Easco Hand Tools, Inc.
Exar Corp.

F

Farragut Mortgage Co.
Fisher Transportation Services, Inc.
Fischer-Watt Gold Co., Inc.

G

Greenwich Financial Corp.
Graphic Packaging Co.
Griffith Consumers Co.
Genzyme Corp.
Groundwater Technology, Inc.
Gartner Group, Inc.

H

Hana Biologicals, Inc.
Henry (Jack) & Associates, Inc.
Heritage Financial Services, Inc.
Huffman Koos, Inc.
Hugh Keith Enterprises, Inc.

FIGURE 3–2. Listing of Substantial New Issues (cont'd.).

Hako Minuteman, Inc.

I

Ideal School Supply Co.
Individual Training Systems, Inc.
Informix
Insituform Gulf South, Inc.
Insituform Mid-America, Inc.
Interface Flooring, Inc.

J

J & J Snack Foods Corp.
Jennifer Convertibles, Inc.
Jiffy Lube International, Inc.
Jones Medical Industries, Inc.

K

Knutson Mortgage Corp.
Krisch American Inns, Inc.

L

Land's End, Inc.
Lakeland Industries, Inc.
Lamberts Pasta & Cheese, Inc.
Lincoln Foodservice Products, Inc.
Liposome Technology, Inc.

M

Machine Vision Int'l Corp.
Marina L.P.
Melamine Chemicals, Inc.
Mail Boxes, Inc.
Markel Corp.
Michael Anthony Stores, Inc.

N

Navigators Group, Inc.
Neeco Corp.
Network Equipment Technologies, Inc.

O

Occupational Medical Corp. of America, Inc.
Old Spaghetti Warehouse, Inc.
Osborne Communications, Inc.
Outlet Communications, Inc.

P

Photronics, Inc.
Polk Audio, Inc.
Pulitzer Publishing, Inc.

R

Rochester Community Savings Bank
Roto-Rooter, Inc.
Reebok International, Ltd.
Regis Corp.

S

SKI, Ltd.
Sun Microsystems, Inc.
Sunresorts Ltd. N.V.

T

TSO Financial

Z

Zeus Components, Inc.

FIGURE 3–3. Listing of Regional Banks, Insurance Companies, and Savings and Loan Associations.

A

Acceptance Insurance Holdings, Inc.
American National Insurance Co.
Amwest Insurance Group, Inc.
American Indemnity/Financial Corp.

B

Business Mens Assurance Corp.
Boston Bancorp.
Boston Five Cents Savings Bank

C

Community Savings Bank
Crawford & Co.

D

Dime Savings Bank (Conn.)
Durham Corp.

E

Equitable of Iowa Co.

F

First Farwest Corp.
Framingham Savings Bank
Fifth Third Bancorporation
First of Long Island Bank

G

Gateway Bank

I

Independence Insurance Group. Inc.

K

Kentucky Central Life Insurance Co.
Kansas City Life Insurance Co.

M

McM Corp.
Marble Financial Corp.

N

National Western Life Insurance Co.
National Security Insurance Co.
New York Marine & Central Insurance Co.

P

Poe & Associates, Inc.
Policy Management Systems Corp.
Preferred Risk Life Insurance Co.

R

Royal Palms Savings Assoc.
Reliable Life Insurance Co.
Rochester Community Savings Bank
Richmond Hill Savings Bank

S

Stifel Financial Corp.
Sooner Federal Savings & Loan, Tulsa
Somerset Bancorporation
Stanford Capital Group
Shawmut Corp.
Southern Security Life Insurance Co.

T

Transworld Bancorporation

U

Unibancorp, Inc.
United Fire & Casualty, Inc.
United Dominion Realty Trust

W

Webster Financial Corp.

similarities and differences among banks, thrifts, and insurance companies. All of these institutions fall under the industry heading "financial services." Such businesses are particularly impacted by factors such as the overall performance of the economy, the level of interest rates, and the trend of the stock market. In the past, the stocks of banks, thrifts, and insurance companies tended to sell at high per-share prices ($50 to $100 or more per share was not uncommon). Ownership rested in the hands of a few major investors and/or local businesspeople and the stocks typically traded within a narrow price range.

The stocks of insurance companies for the most part continue to hold to the foregoing pattern, but the stocks of banks and thrifts do not. Many thrifts have converted from mutual to stock associations and have priced their offerings relatively modestly to attract the interest of their depositors and induce them to become shareholders. Also, the recent trend toward interstate banking has resulted in many regional banks and savings and loan associations being absorbed by larger institutions.

The aforementioned factors have resulted in a marked drop in the average price at which banks and savings and loan associations trade. Hence, they are more interesting to the average investor. Also, these factors have resulted in more volatile price movements, particularly among those banks and savings and loans subject to takeovers.

Now that you have a general understanding of some of the trends and typical patterns for these types of stocks, you can turn to some strategies for selecting those stocks that might represent appropriate investments for you.

Evaluating Banks and Thrifts

Appendix III describes in some detail the key ratios and techniques used in financial analysis, and you are encouraged to study that material carefully. This section identifies those ratios that are of special significance when deciding whether the stock of a particular bank or thrift represents a buy, sell, or hold.

Book value is the first item to consider: You can normally find the stock's book value highlighted in the bank or thrift's annual report. Concentrate your efforts on those institutions selling in the marketplace at a substantial discount from their book value. Consider why such a situation exists. If you determine that the reason for this situation simply reflects the fact that market professionals have not discovered the particular bank or thrift, you may indeed have identified an undervalued stock. On the other hand, you may find that the stock's low price represents unskilled or indifferent management. (*See* Chapter 5.) In that case, the stock is probably not worth your investment.

Once you identify such a truly discounted bank or thrift, turn your attention to the percentage of nonoperating assets to total assets. This ratio tells you what proportion of the institution's loans are in default, that is, not earning interest (hence the term nonoperating). Those institutions with the lowest ratio of nonoperating assets are the most desirable. Examples of nonoperating assets include such things as foreign loans (a particular problem of money-center banks, though some regional banks participated in such loans) and real estate foreclosures (a possible problem for thrifts located in poor economic areas of the country).

Finally, consider the geographic area the particular bank or thrift operates in. Having branches located in an affluent community (or communities) would add to the worth of the thrift in question and increase the likelihood of its being taken over. But don't reject any financial institution located in a depressed area such as the "oil patch" on that fact alone. The stock price may be overly depressed compared to book value and nonoperating assets.

While the foregoing are the three most important factors to be considered in connection with banks and thrifts, other particulars, such as deposit structure (amount of time versus savings deposits), capital structure, earnings trend, and return on assets should be considered before you invest in a particular financial institution.

Types of Insurance Companies

For the most part, regional insurance companies—as opposed to national companies—are traded over the counter. Life and health insurance companies represent a more significant factor in the OTC marketplace in terms of the number of companies and their asset size, but you can also find over-the-counter property and casualty insurance companies that present the opportunity to buy assets at a discount.

It is important to realize that the insurance industry is really two industries in one: property and casualty insurance and life and health insurance. Before you analyze any insurance company you need to understand the key characteristics of these two distinct sectors of the insurance industry.

Typically, the earnings and assets of property and casualty insurance companies are subject to greater swings than those of life and health insurance companies. For one thing, catastrophes such as hurricanes, tornadoes, and the like—and the resultant costs to insurers—are impossible to predict. In addition, the property and casualty insurance industry has been subject to periods of intense competition during which little, if any, concern for the bottom line—earnings figures—was apparent.

After citing the aforementioned negative factors about property and casualty insurance companies, why should any investor be interested in this category of OTC stock? First, by utilizing the tools described in Appendix III, you should be able to identify those property and casualty companies that are most effective in controlling their risk and expense ratios before they are discovered by professional investors. Second, the marketplace tends to overreach—either excessively marking up or down in price a particular category of stock. Buying property and casualty companies at the bottom of a cycle may prove very rewarding when the pendulum swings in the opposite direction.

Life and health insurance companies, on the other hand, have for the most part enjoyed a pattern of stable and, in some instances, uneventful growth in terms of earnings and assets.

The overall pattern has been much less erratic than that of the property and casualty companies.

How to Select a "Bargain" Among Insurance Stocks

To find an insurance company that represents a real opportunity, begin by looking first at book value, as we did for banks and thrifts. Once you have determined that an insurance company is selling below book value, spend some additional time trying to determine why.

Next, examine the rate at which premiums are expanding. Growth in premiums is a way of gauging a company's success in marketing its products. Also consider the level of underwriting reserves. This ratio determines how much new business an insurance company can take on, and thus the company's growth potential.

"SMOKESTACK AMERICA"— REGIONAL AND THINLY TRADED COMPANIES

"Smokestack America" stocks generally represent regional, inactively traded companies whose products are mainly industrial in nature. For these reasons, the names of such companies ordinarily are not household words. In fact, most investors, both individual and professional, are unfamiliar with the majority of "smokestack America" companies listed in Figure 3–4. For this reason, some of the best buys among over-the-counter securities can be found among the smokestack-type companies.

Advantages of Investing in Regional Companies

What makes regional companies attractive for you, the individual investor, is that you can often find undiscovered value among those stocks. These firms are not well known: They are often traded via the pink sheets and not listed with NASDAQ, either because their managements did not seek a

FIGURE 3–4. Listing of "Smokestack America" Companies.

A

Adrian Steel Co.
Atlantic City Sewerage Co.
Allied Security, Inc.
Anderson-Tully Co.

C

Conbraco Industries Inc.
Consolidated Tomolka Land Co.

D

Daniel Green Co.
Dominquez Water Co.
Dundee Mills, Inc.

F

Farmers Brothers, Inc.
Finnigan Corp.
Fownes Bros., Inc.
Frawley Corp.

G

General Builders, Inc.
Genesee Corp. "B"
Goody Products, Inc.
Gray Communication Systems, Inc.
Gyrodyne Corporation of America, Inc.

K

Kahler Corp.
Keweenaw Land Assoc. CTF Int.
Kreisler Mfg. Co.

L

Lexington & 42nd Street (Chanin Building)
Liverpool Industries, Inc.

M

Benjamin Moore Paint Co.
J. Michael, Inc.
Manischewitz, Inc.
Manitowoc Corp.
Marina Ltd. Ptn.
Maui Land & Pineapple Co.
Mills Music Trust—Units
Mischer, Inc.
Molokai Ranch, Inc.

P

Paxton (Frank) Company
Preformed Line Products, Inc.

S

St. Joe Paper Co.
Service Fracturing Co.
Simpson Timber Co.
Spartan Mills, Inc.
Square Industries, Inc.
Stauffer Communications Co.
Supradur Products, Inc.
Supreme Equipment & Mfg. Co.
William Sadlier, Inc.

T

Tecumseh Products, Inc.
Tennant Co.
Thermal National, Inc.
Tower Properties, Inc.
Trus Joist, Inc.

V

Vallen Corp.
Vermillion Bay Land Co.

W

Weisfields, Inc.
Woodward Governor, Inc.

Y

Young's Market, Inc.

NASDAQ listing or because the companies do not qualify—typically because they have relatively few public shareholders. Further, many regional companies occupy dominant positions within the industry or market niche: They may be a major force and employer in the particular city or town in which they are located. The managements of many smokestack companies are conservative in their approach toward business, a fact that is reflected in strong balance sheets, excess funding in pension plans, and the stable manner in which their stocks are traded. All of the foregoing characteristics make "smokestack America" companies likely takeover candidates once they are identified by professional investors.

Finding Attractive Candidates

If some regional smokestack companies that are relatively unknown represent real buying opportunities, how can you, as an investor, identify them? One way is to subscribe to an investment advisory service or newsletter that specializes in locating such companies. (Appendix I contains a detailed listing of advisory services and newsletters with capsule descriptions of the kinds of over-the-counter stocks they analyze.) A second way might be for you to become active in such organizations as the American Association of Individual Investors, Inc. located at 625 North Michigan Avenue, Chicago, IL 60611 (312-280-0170). This association provides an opportunity for you to meet and exchange investment ideas with other individual investors through monthly meetings of local chapters, as well as a monthly newsletter, correspondence courses, and special interest groups. Joining an investment club in your particular locale can also bring to your attention regional companies that you may not be personally familiar with. And, of course, as an individual investor you should constantly be on the alert for information about local companies that have facilities in your immediate area and whose activities may be carried in local newspapers or may be the subject of conversation among friends and family members employed by such firms.

Evaluating Their Potential

If something interests you about a local company, go one step further and obtain a copy of its annual report. Consider the value of the company's assets, both with regard to their present use or their value if they were liquidated or put to an alternative use. Remember that many regional companies have relatively few shares outstanding in public hands and hence are thinly traded, so it may be difficult to build up a significant position or to liquidate one that has been built up. Find out the stock's float and spread so you are clear just how liquid—or illiquid—the stock is.

Particularly in the case of regional companies, attending the annual meeting of shareholders—almost all of whom are either local residents and/or employees—can give you a real insight into the direction the company is heading and what, if any, consideration the company gives its outside shareholders.

Evaluating Smokestack Companies

Once you have examined the annual report and attended the shareholders' meeting, if you find the firm still interests you, you need to make a financial analysis. The significant ratios and techniques are presented in Appendix III. How significant is "number crunching" in the case of the smokestack companies? As with blue chip stocks, banks and insurance companies, and substantial new issues, sound financial analysis is essential. Concentrate on the balance sheet or asset side of regional companies (as opposed to income statement or growth side of such companies). Direct your attention and effort toward those ratios that bring into focus the balance sheet strengths or weaknesses of the company. The reason for concentrating on the aforementioned ratios is your interest in identifying opportunities to buy physical assets at a discount—that exists particularly in the case of regional smokestack-type companies. The current ratio, the quick ratio, and the book value would be the first to calculate in the case of a smokestack-type company. But do not ignore completely the income statement or growth side of regional companies. Instead, calculate the company's return-on-assets ratio. If this should prove substantially higher than the industry norm or for industries generally, you may want to consider whether the company may indeed be a potential Xerox or IBM of the future. Bear in mind that both these companies started out as unknown regional companies traded over the counter.

4

Trading in More Speculative Stocks

The foregoing chapter described in some detail the categories of stocks favored by so-called "investors." Such stocks are generally those of stable, well-capitalized firms whose financials provide the potential investor with considerable information. This chapter describes some of the more speculative OTC stocks, including those of start-up companies, bankrupt companies, and foreign firms, as well as penny stocks. It is important you realize that, although these stocks may carry relatively high risk/reward ratios or may be more difficult to evaluate than the more conservative stocks, with proper research and preparation they are *not* gambles. Rather, they offer legitimate, and often excellent, opportunities to the knowledgeable individual. This chapter aims to help you take advantage of these opportunities.

START-UP OPERATIONS

As discussed in Chapter 3, new issues of stock represent two types of companies: substantial companies and start-up operations. Substantial companies generally have large earnings, assets, and capitalization and a track record for you to examine. Such issues are commonly underwritten by large, well-known brokerage firms, and although the performance of the new issue is likely helped by its having a major underwriter, the company's financials are far more significant in determining the stock's performance.

A start-up company, on the other hand, has little in the way of assets, earnings, and the like, so you have very little to work with or to which you can apply the number crunching techniques. In this case the crucial ingredient can be summed up in one work—sponsorship. To a large measure you have to rely on the reputation of the company's underwriter—how successful the underwriter has been in the past in selecting companies that have grown and prospered and how active the underwriter is in getting the company's story told.

A word of caution: Unless you, as an investor, are personally knowledgeable about a particular new technology or scientific development or unless you are a substantial and sophisticated investor, you may be wise to avoid investing in start-up situations. Analyzing underwriter sponsorship can be difficult, as in most instances a start-up company is taken public by a small brokerage firm with limited capital and customer base. And remember, always be cautious about investing in *any* situation brought to your attention by a cold call.

THE STOCKS OF BANKRUPT COMPANIES

The stocks of bankrupt companies is a category of OTC stock followed by very few professional and individual investors. For this very reason it offers the astute investor opportunities for substantial profits. Just why are so few investors willing to invest in this area of the over-the-counter marketplace? For one thing, institutional investors in particular are precluded by law or by institutional practice from investing in such "risky" securities. Second, many investors feel inadequate to analyze bankrupt situations or are simply unwilling to expend any effort in this special market niche. This section should familiarize you with the basic techniques needed to analyze a bankrupt stock and give you the confidence to do just that in a real-life situation.

A Practical Example

Perhaps the best way to illustrate the potential profitability of investing in a bankruptcy situation is to cite a real-life example. At the outset, the point should be made that investments in bankruptcy situations require skill and effort and that not all produce the same level of return as did the following situation. Bearing these caveats in mind, let's proceed to discuss our real-life situation.

Interstate Stores, Inc. (Interstate) was an operating and profitable discount chain into the early 1970s. In the course of conducting its discount business, Interstate acquired a toy retailer. This toy retailer had developed a revolutionary marketing approach, with resulting geometrical growth in sales and earnings. However, the toy division's approach was not enough to prevent the parent company's (Interstate) bankruptcy when the discount business went into a slump.

Shortly after declaring bankruptcy, Interstate's stock traded for as little as one-eighth of a dollar and most investors lost interest in the company as it wound its way through the bankruptcy courts. But a few astute investors continued to follow the company because of its highly successful retailing toy division. At the time Interstate came out of bankruptcy, the man who was the driving force of the toy division became president of the revitalized company. Such is the history of Toys R Us, Inc. The few astute investors who bought into it while it was in bankruptcy saw the stock go from one-eighth of a dollar per share to $60 or more per share.

Two important lessons can be learned from this example. First, even bankrupt companies often have valuable assets. For that matter, some bankruptcies are merely the result of such short-term occurrences as disasters, lawsuits, or illiquid assets (that is, lack of cash flow). Interstate's bankruptcy contained an element common to many bankruptcy situations:

One or more divisions of a company contributed to its fall into bankruptcy while other divisions remained profitable and healthy.

Second, although the bankruptcy of a major company typically makes financial headlines when it occurs, the bankrupt company and its stock disappear from public view in a short time. Only by carefully following the whole bankruptcy proceeding can you determine if the company has any substantial assets that are unrecognized by other investors and whether the company is likely to come out of bankruptcy and return to profitability.

Identifying Promising Bankrupt Companies

Figure 4–1 lists a number of companies that are presently in bankruptcy and whose stocks are trading over the counter. Beyond that, you can simply make it your practice to regularly follow up the major and minor bankruptcies reported in the financial pages. Appendix I includes the major financial services and newsletters that track major and minor bankruptcies and advise their readers of the best investment opportunities. By subscribing to these services you buy a "screening service" that helps focus your attention on a few bankrupt stocks that warrant further evaluation and analysis. (Remember that the purpose of any advisory service is to bring you ideas, but the task of evaluating those ideas and determining which offer the best opportunities remains yours.)

Evaluating Bankruptcies

Once you have focused on a particular bankrupt stock you are left with the question of where to find the information you need about the company. After an initial headline about the bankruptcy of a major firm, investors typically lose interest and coverage moves from the front page to the back page of the financial section. As an individual investor, you need to contact the bankrupt company's counsel and request that your name be added to the list of interested parties (that is, the list of existing shareholders, creditors, and suppliers) who receive copies of court proceedings, news releases, and other documents relating to the bankruptcy. You need these documents to evaluate whether the particular bankrupt stock is worth investing in.

Once on the mailing list, you will be kept informed of such things as creditor committee meetings; proposed plans for reorganizing the company and taking it out of bankruptcy; and periodic statements as to the financial condition of the bankrupt company. From the factual/narrative material sent to you as an interested party you should be able to determine whether the creditors and management of the bankrupt company are working well together and how easy or difficult it will be for a proposed plan of reorganization to be developed, submitted, and approved by all parties to the bankruptcy.

Using the financial data and the various analytical tools described in Appendix III, you should be able to identify the factors that led to the company's bankruptcy. The reasons might be something as simple as a cash flow problem resulting from illiquid or mismanaged short-term assets to much more serious problems such as loss of market share or foreign competition—to name just a few of the possible reasons a company may file for bankruptcy. Further, from the financial data presented you should be able to develop a "feel" for the financial condition of the company as it proceeds through the reorganization process. For instance, you may determine from its financials that the company is accumulating large cash assets that are not reflected in the price of the company's outstanding bonds or stock. For example, the bonds of a certain bankrupt real estate company were selling at a 50% discount (that is, $500 for each $1000 bond), but during the course of its reorganization the company had accumulated enough cash to pay off the bonds in full as well as to distribute preferred shares to its bondholders. Further, the bankrupt company's financials should enable you to identify the value of any remaining assets it owns, for example, any value attached to its name, i.e., consumer franchise. Finally, from the narrative and financial material supplied to interested parties you

FIGURE 4–1. Listing of Bankrupt Companies.

Such companies are denoted with the symbol "VJ" in the pink sheets.

A

Advanced Logic Systems, Inc.
Altec Corp.
American Bloodpressure Centers, Inc.
American Solar King Corp.
Argonaut Energy Corp.
Atco Industries, Inc.

B

Bedford Computer Corp.
Bell Natl Corp.
Boro Recycling, Inc.

C

Cable Applications, Inc.
Care Enterprises, Inc.
Chargit, Inc.
Coastal Industries, Inc.
Conesco Industries Ltd. A

D

Disc Technology Corp.
Discovery Oil Ltd.

E

E Tron Corp.
Eastern York, Inc.
Enchanted Village, Inc.

F

First Hartford Corp.
Frier Industries, Inc.
Frigitemp Corp.

G

Gascard Club, Inc.
Geophysical Physical Systems Corp.

H

Harrell Intl., Inc.
Hydodyne Industries, Inc.

I

Int'l Institute of Applied Technology, Inc.

J

Jamco Ltd.

FIGURE 4–1. Listing of Bankrupt Companies (cont'd.).

K

Kaiser Steel, Inc.
Key Energy Enterprises, Inc.
Key Image Systems, Inc.

L

Life Imaging Corp.

M

Mansfield Tire & Rubber Co.
Martha Manning Co., Inc.
Master Security Services, Inc.
Melridge, Inc.
Midland Capital Corp.
Midwestern Companies
Munson Geothermal, Inc.
Murphy Industries, Inc.

N

New York City Shoes, Inc.

O

ORS Automated, Inc.
Omni-Wave Electronics, Inc.
Osgrow Products Corp.
Oxi Oil Corp.

P

Phaser Systems, Inc.
Pizza Time Theatre, Inc.
Potter Instrument Co.
Public Service of New Hampshire, Inc.
Pyro-Magnetics Corp.

Q

Quaker City Industries, Inc.

R

Radice Corp.
Rayne Industries, Inc.
Reading Industries, Inc.
Richmond Tank Car, Inc.
Royale Airlines, Inc.

S

Santec Corp.
Sharon Steel Corp.
Southern Biotech, Inc.
Spencer Companies, Inc.
Swiss Chalet, Inc.

V

Vector Graphics, Inc.

W

Wincom Corp.
Winn Enterprises, Inc.

should be able to decide how long it will take for a plan of reorganization to be developed and implemented, if indeed it appears likely the company can be reorganized at all. After reviewing all these factors, you should be in a position to determine whether the particular bankrupt stock represents an appropriate investment opportunity.

What About Return?

Obviously the anticipated rate of return should be high before you consider investing in any bankruptcy situation. An annualized return of at least 50% of the amount invested is the least you should expect before investing in a bankrupt company. A number of factors justify requiring such a high return. For one thing, a measure of risk is connected with investing in such situations. Although the techniques and tools described in the foregoing should help to reduce risk, investing in bankrupt companies is not appropriate for everyone. In addition, the payout period in a bankruptcy situation may be two, three, or more years, so that you may have your money tied up—not earning interest—for some time. Such investments require patience. Finally, because you cannot purchase bankrupt stocks on margin you are precluded from using this crucial tool to magnify your gains. Therefore, look for a high rate of return from every dollar committed to investments in bankrupt companies.

Diversification

As an alternative to investing only in specific bankruptcy situations, you might consider investing in a "package" of such securities. Rather than commit all your available funds to one bankruptcy situation, you can invest in a number of such situations. With this approach, you can reduce your risk through diversification as well as assure a steady income stream as the bankruptcy situations unwind over a staggered period of time. Another alternative is to invest in a mutual fund that specializes in bankruptcy and liquidation situations. Such a fund offers the advantages of skilled management and diversification. For example, the Mutual Series of Funds (c/o Herzog, Heine Geduld, Inc., 51 John F. Kennedy Pkwy., Short Hills, NJ 07678/1-800-448-3863) specializes in identifying and investing in bankruptcy and liquidation situations. It is left to you, the reader, to contact these funds and decide which, if any, meet your investment goals.

FOREIGN STOCKS

Historically, the over-the-counter market has been the trading place for foreign securities. With the development of the American Depository Receipt (ADR) and in recent years the trend toward internationalization of the securities markets, investor interest in foreign securities has mushroomed. Today, stocks of many of the world's leading companies are traded over the counter as both individual and institutional investors look to participate in the growth opportunities available to astute investors.

ADRs: Simplifying Foreign Investing

In the past, trading in foreign securities was made difficult by the fact that many foreign countries prohibit direct ownership by non-citizens of shares of their public corporations. Investing abroad was further complicated by the fact that it might take weeks to effect a reregistration of certificates from old owner to new owner when such reregistration was initiated in the United States and when the foreign company's transfer agent is located in the country of origin—which had been the usual practice. Such a situation is unacceptable in our highly liquid securities markets.

ADRs were created to help alleviate these problems. An American Depository Receipt is actually a new security, "created" by a U.S. bank with overseas offices and foreign correspondents. The new security represents shares of the underlying foreign stock physically held in the possession of a U.S. bank overseas.

"Morgan Guaranty Trust Company, N.A. and Citibank Corporation, N.A. are typical of such banking institutions. Each bank acts as an intermediary between the foreign company's transfer agent and the U.S. investor. Each is empowered to transfer ownership of the ADRs on its books and records but continues as the official holder of record on the company's stockholder list. The actual foreign shares remain registered in the name of the bank while under the control of the bank. Of course, investors can always exchange ADRs for the underlying common stock if they choose to do so, but this is rarely the case except among international traders who often need the comparable security to satisfy contractual commitments here or abroad."[1]

Certain other features of ADRs are important for an understanding of how foreign securities are traded in the over-the-counter marketplace. American Depository Receipts come in various denominations and represent the foreign stock share-for-share, with one major exception. In the case of Japanese securities, one ADR is typically equal to ten underlying shares. Also, while in the past ADRs were issued principally in connection with English, Swiss, German, and South African companies, in recent years there has been an ever-growing number of ADRs issued in connection with companies domiciled in Japan, Korea, Hong Kong, and European countries such as Norway and Sweden. Such a pattern of interest in an ever-growing diversity of foreign companies serves to support the argument that the over-the-counter market in foreign securities is becoming ever more international in scope.

Rights of Ownership

ADRs are subject to SEC regulation within the United States. For this reason, holders of ADRs are entitled to full protection under the laws of the United States as well as to most of the advantages of stock ownership accorded investors

[1]Pessin, Allan H., *The Illustrated Encyclopedia of the Securities Industry*, New York Institute of Finance, 1988, p. 12-13.

in domestic securities. For example, for an ADR to be created, the foreign corporation must agree to furnish audited financials, including an audited annual report containing a balance sheet and income statement, to all holders of its ADRs. This requirement has been a major impetus behind the trend of foreign corporations to supply their shareholders with more detailed information as to assets, earnings, and future plans. While the concepts of disclosure and investors' rights may vary from country to country, they are recognized by virtually all countries in the Free World. In addition, holders of ADRs are entitled to receive cash dividends, stock dividends and splits, subscription rights, and voting privileges.

Selecting Foreign Stocks

Figure 4–2 lists foreign stocks traded over the counter. Figure 4–3 lists market makers who specialize in foreign securities. How do you choose from among these stocks?

In evaluating the suitability of any foreign OTC stock, first consider the situation of the country where the company is domiciled. How stable is the country politically, and how strong is its economy? Is its currency likely to be devalued and, if so, by how much? What (if anything) makes the country an attractive place to invest in?

Another facet to examine is the industry or industries the company operates in. In analyzing the company itself, use the information and techniques presented in Appendix III. Beyond that, it is important for you, as an investor, to realize that although most foreign companies are moving toward greater disclosure of financial and other corporate information, some have moved more rapidly than others. Depending on the tax environment it operates in, a foreign company may seek to hide its true earnings, and in some instances getting an accurate picture of the company's earnings may be extremely difficult.

For this reason most analysts of foreign securities concentrate on a company's balance sheet as opposed to its income statement, giving substantial weight to a foreign company's book value and asset structure. But even this precaution is not foolproof; many analysts feel that foreign companies understate their assets for fear of attracting unwanted corporate suitors. In addition, the class system and close family affiliations that exist in many foreign countries encourage managements to view their companies as private fiefdoms. As a result, some corporate insiders see nothing wrong with seeking personal gain at the expense of the corporation. In the same vein, many foreign countries permit what in the United States would be considered insider trading and place little if any restrictions on transactions by corporate officers.

Risk and Reward

In light of these considerations, is it worth your while to invest in foreign stocks traded over the counter? The answer is that it can be. As with bankrupt stocks, the returns from investing in foreign stock can be 50% or more on an annualized basis for the capital invested. But likewise, the risks attached to investing in foreign securities are higher. The purpose of highlighting the difficulties of evaluating foreign stocks bring home to you, the reader, the fact that investing in foreign securities requires you to spend the time and effort to familiarize yourself with any foreign company you are considering investing in. While the effort is more than would be required for investing in certain other categories of stocks traded over the counter, the rewards can be substantially higher.

Alternatives

For the individual investor who does not wish to invest in specific foreign equities or who is unwilling or unable to spend time identifying particular stocks, a number of alternatives are available. Closed-end funds that invest in particular

FIGURE 4–2. Listing of Foreign Stocks Traded Over the Counter.

A

Anglo-American South African ADR
Anglo-American Gold Inv ADR
Asea AB ADR

B

Beecham Group ADR
Blyvoor Gold Mng ADR
Bowater Industries PLC ADR
Buffeisfontein Gold Mng ADR
BanPonce Corp.
Banco Popular de PR

C

Corby Distillers
Cambrian & General Securities PLC
Compania Tel Nac'l ADR

D

Daily Mail & General Trust PLC

E

Elan Corp. PLC ADS

F

Free States Consolidated Gold Mines ADR

H

Hard Rock Int'l ADR

I

Instrumentarium "B" ADR
Ito Yokado LTD ADR

L

Lonrho Ltd.

M

Matsushita El Ind ADR
Montedison SPO ADS

O

Oce-van der Griten ADR

P

Pharmacia AB ADR

T

Tokio Marine & Fire, Inc. ADR
Telefonos de Mexico ADR

U

Unilever NV
United Newspapers ADR

V

Vaal Reefs Ex & Mng ADR
Volvo AB ADR

W

Western Deep Levels, ADR

FIGURE 4–3. Listing of Market Makers Specializing in Foreign Securities.

Arnhold & S Bleichroeder Inc.
Carl Marx & Co.
Daiwa Securities Inc.
Deutsche Bank Capital Corp.
Eberstadt Fleming Inc.
First Boston Co.
Goldman Sachs & Co.
Morgan Stanley & Co.
Nikko Securities Co. Intl Inc.
Nomura Securities Intl Inc. N.Y.
Prudential Bache Securities Inc.
Shearson Lehman Hutton, Inc.
UBS Securities Inc.
S.G. Warburg Rowe & Pitman Akroyd Inc.
Yamachi Intl Inc.

countries represent one possibility. Global funds—funds that invest in the securities of any number of foreign countries—have become increasingly popular and in some instances have been the best-performing funds over the past few years. Figure 4–4 lists both country and global funds.

PENNY STOCKS

In the minds of many investors, the concept of the OTC market has been linked to the low-priced penny stocks. By now you probably realize that penny stocks account for only a small portion of over-the-counter trading and that the over-the-counter marketplace provides a home for a diversity of stocks. With that understanding, let's take a look at the traditional category of "penny" stocks.

Penny stocks are generally defined as those issues selling at $5 per share or below. A per share price of $5 or lower is significant because stocks selling at that price have limited marginability and because a number of the major brokerage firms discourage customer purchases of such low-priced stocks. For this latter reason, you need to take extra time to

FIGURE 4–4. Listing of Country and Global Funds.

- First Australia Fund
- France Fund
- Germany Fund
- Helvetia Fund
- Italy Fund
- Japan Fund
- Mexico Fund
- Korea Fund
- Taiwan Fund
- Templeton Emerging Markets Fund and Other Templeton Off Shore Funds
- Scandinavia Fund
- Scudder New Asia Fund and Other Scudder Off Shore Funds

locate a particular firm and registered representative to handle your transactions in penny stocks.

Tracking Your Penny Stocks

The prices of penny stocks are the most volatile of all stocks traded OTC and hence you need to check their price action frequently with your broker. This is just one reason you need to select the right brokerage firm and registered representative when you invest in penny stocks.

For a penny stock to be traded via NASDAQ, a minimum bid price of at least $3 per share is required at the outset. A NASDAQ listing carries with it a four-letter symbol that when typed into a terminal enables the investor to obtain an instantaneous quote on the stock and hence gives the stock added visibility. Also, because NASDAQ releases to the media quotations on its stocks (as described in Chapter 1, page 23), you, the investor, can monitor your NASDAQ-listed stocks daily.

On the other hand, the majority of penny stocks are not listed via NASDAQ, but that fact need not preclude your investing in such stocks. It just means that you have to rely on your broker to obtain quotes for you either by checking the day's pink sheets and giving you the prior day's prices or by calling the market makers and obtaining a fresh quote for you.

Identifying Appropriate Penny Stocks

To select penny stocks for investment you can use three different approaches.

One approach is to simply "scan" all of the low-priced stocks quoted in the pink sheets. This approach is used by many professional traders and market makers to identify additional stocks to make markets in. Although this approach is extremely time-consuming—requiring you to view investing as a serious avocation—scanning the pink sheets can lead you to uncovering a particular penny stock before it is discovered by market professionals. Further, as discussed in Chapter 2, scanning the pink sheets makes you more familiar with the names of the various market makers and the types of stocks they make markets in. Then, when you see their names in the financial papers, you have a better understanding of how they are viewed by the financial community—unfavorably or favorably. Over time you will develop a feel as to how a particular OTC stock trades on the basis of the type of brokerage firm making a market in its stock.

Another way to identify particular penny stocks is by subscribing to one or more investment advisory services that specialize in the penny-stock market. Appendix I lists some major services, along with descriptions of the information they provide. Basically all these services provide a screen to narrow down the universe of penny stocks. But you, the investor, need to do more than simply rely on their recommendations. Apply the financial analysis tools and techniques described in Appendix III to determine if the particular penny stock represents an appropriate investment. Remember that many advisory services operate from their own viewpoint and have no concept of your individual financial position or your attitude towards risk.

The third and perhaps most important technique for identifying penny stocks for investment is locating a broker who combines character and ability and whose approach to investing matches your own. The following checklist presents some key factors to consider when selecting a broker and/or brokerage firm to handle your investments in penny stocks.

1. Realize that your interests and those of your broker may conflict. The broker's income is generated from the commissions on the stocks bought and sold through his or her efforts—particularly in the case of penny stocks. Don't hesitate to hold off giving your broker a trade. Also, be sure the firm and the broker you deal with are in compliance with all regulatory authorities.
2. As a general rule, invest only with a broker who has a track record in the business. Two years is generally the minimum experience you should require of any broker handling penny stocks. Likewise, the firm employing the broker you select should have a minimum of two to five years in the business. In the penny stock market, the turnover of both brokers and firms is high, so be sure the firm has staying power.
3. Does your prospective broker do his or her own research? Rather than merely listen to a sales pitch, ask what the recommendation is based on and request a copy of the research report and the company's Form 10K and Annual Report. Look at the numbers for yourself—when you are away from the broker's sales pitch.
4. Consider the market-making role of the firm employing your prospective broker. Is the firm the lead market maker of the recommended stock or merely one in the crowd? The position of the firm determines how easily you can acquire and dispose of stock as well as how steep the spread between bid and asked prices will be.
5. Determine for yourself how close your prospective broker and his or her firm are to the particular penny stock recommended. On the one hand, you want the relationship close enough so that the broker is aware of what occurs at the company, but not so close that the firm is acting as agent for the penny-stock company.

6. Be especially careful when dealing with cold callers and avoid dealing with high-pressure types of brokers and the firms employing them.

Analyzing Your Selections

Unlike many categories of over-the-counter stocks for which number crunching plays a major role in analysis, penny stocks depend largely on sponsorship. Which market maker is behind the stock and which advisory firms recommend the particular penny stock are crucial factors in determining how the stock will perform in the future. This fact is basic to investing in penny stocks and is something you as an investor should realize. Additionally, look for a penny stock with a "story" attached to it. Is the company in the forefront of a scientific discovery, a marketing trend, or a public fad? Unlike most other categories of stocks traded over the counter, a particular penny stock may move out of investor favor just as rapidly as it moved into the spotlight.

Beyond these general considerations, certain mechanical strategies may prove helpful when investing in penny stocks. First, any penny stock bought at the beginning of a popularity cycle (that is, at a low price) should be liquidated at the first sign of any drop-off (decline) in price. As with any mechanical rule there is an exception: If you are personally knowledgeable, and convinced from independent analysis that the particular penny stock represents a unique opportunity to get in on the ground floor of a revolutionary product or industry, you may appropriately retain the stock. A second strategy is to sell any stock that reaches a predetermined level: for example, two, three, or more times its original purchase price.

From the foregoing, you can see that penny stocks can be a difficult arena to invest in. In addition, certain other categories of over-the-counter stocks, particularly bankrupt stocks and new issues, might by definition fall into the category of penny stocks. When looking at any penny stock, always consider whether the company has hard numbers and in-depth management or whether the venture is highly speculative—

FIGURE 4–5. Listing of Penny Stocks—Stocks Selling at $5 or Lower.

A

Academy Insurance Co.
ADAC Laboratories, Inc.
Alaska Apollo Gold Mines
Alexander Energy Co.
American Solar King, Inc.
Arabian Shield Dev Corp.
Avino Mines & Resources, Inc.

B

Barton Industries, Inc.
Bellwether Explorations, Inc.
Business Cards Tomorrow, Inc.

C

C.A. Blockers, Inc.
CACI Int'l Class A
Cardiac Control Systems, Inc.
Care Plus, Inc.
Cellular Products, Inc.
Central Reserve Life Insurance Co.
Citizens Security Group
Clinical Data, Inc.
Cobb Resources Corp.
CPT Corp.
Cypertek, Inc.

D

Dewey Electronics, Inc.
DH Technology, Inc.

E

Ehrlich Bober Financial, Inc.
Electro Catheter, Inc.
Enscor, Inc.
Equity Oil, Inc.

F

Fibronics, Inc.
Fingermatrix, Inc.

G

Grease Monkey Holding Co.
Greenwood Holdings, Inc.

I

Intermagnetics General, Inc.

J

Jack Carl/312 Futures, Inc.
Johnstown American, Inc.

K

KenCope Energy, Inc.

L

Palmer G. Lewis, Inc.
Life of Indiana, Inc.
Lincoln Logs, Inc.

M

Machine Technology, Inc.
Mischer Corp.

T

Tom Brown, Inc.
TS Industries, Inc.
TSR, Inc.

U

Universal Security Instruments, Inc.
Universal Voltronics, Inc.

V

Vie de France, Inc.
Vulcan Packing, Inc.

Z

Zygad, Inc.

as are the majority of penny stocks traded over the counter. An evaluation of its sponsorship is the crucial element in determining whether or not you should invest in a particular penny stock.

The level of return to look for from penny stocks is high—on the order of 50% or better on an annualized basis for all capital committed to such equities. As an individual investor, you should determine at the outset how much of your capital would be appropriately invested in penny stocks. Many investors treat what they invest in penny stocks as "play money" and limit to 10% or less the amount invested in this category of stock.

With penny stocks, you should always be alert to the spread between bid and asked prices and closely monitor price and volume changes. Investing in penny stocks requires you to be ready and able to make rapid decisions—particularly when it comes to liquidating such stocks. Figure 4–5 lists "penny" stocks currently traded over the counter.

As you have seen in these chapters, over-the-counter investments encompass a wide variety of stocks, and keeping track of the relevant information about your OTC stocks could become a major avocation. If this is for you, the next chapter should help you to sift through the published materials, to use personal contacts, and to approach the managements of OTC companies. On the other hand, if you feel that picking your own stocks requires more time and effort than you care to commit at this time, the next chapter introduces you to some of the alternatives—professionally managed mutual funds that invest over the counter.

5

Managing Your Own Investment Program or Leaving It to the Pros

As an individual investor, you can choose to select and manage your own OTC stocks or you can invest in mutual funds that specialize in such stocks. In either case, you should be familiar with the sources of information professionals use and with some of the principal types of funds available. This chapter presents a professional approach to stock selection and can help you decide whether to invest on your own or through the medium of a fund.

What are some of the pros and cons to acting as your own stock picker? Managing your own investments gives you better control of your own destiny. No one understands your risk tolerance, for example, better than you do. As an individual investor, you are free to invest in any stock you identify as undervalued, whether it is thinly traded or low priced, whereas an institutional investor might be prohibited from tracking a stock because of liquidity considerations or fund objectives.

On the other hand, mutual funds specializing in OTC stocks offer the advantage of less risk simply by virtue of greater diversification. A fund also provides professional management and saves time—important considerations to the individual who has neither the time nor the inclination to do investment research.

Deciding whether to invest on your own or via a fund is a personal decision.

IF YOU DO IT YOURSELF ...

Market Publications You Should Follow

Basic information about public companies is found in publications such as Standard & Poor's, Moodys, and Value Line. Both S&P and Moodys report in their daily news sections virtually all corporate news and, in volumes listing companies in alphabetical order, complete descriptions of a corporation's history, capital structure, management, principal shareholders, stock price range, and current financials. In addition to these basic publications, S&P and Moodys publish monthly pocket-sized, soft-covered guides listing by company name the most recent financial information on virtually all publicly traded stocks and bonds. Standard and Poor's also publishes a "Register of Corporations, Directors, and Executives," which can be especially useful in learning more about thinly traded, regional companies. Virtually all the information in S&P and Moodys publications is now available on database, with specially designed software programs to help you identify those OTC stocks offering exceptional investment opportunities.

Value Line takes a somewhat different tack in treating both listed and OTC stocks. First, it covers only select companies, the majority of which are listed. The most important OTC stocks are included as well. Second, it provides an excellent overview of various industry groupings such as autos, steel, computers, and so forth and gives a detailed appraisal of the significant factors affecting particular companies. Utilizing its own scale, Value Line rates companies in terms of safety, short- and long-term prospects, and income using evaluation techniques developed and refined over a long time.

Obviously publications such as the *Wall Street Journal, Investors Daily, Forbes,* and *Barrons* (to name just a few) are "must" reading for the serious investor. But although headline stories and articles are useful, your best investment ideas may be gleaned from passing comments and references to lesser-known, small-cap companies typically traded over the counter. A growing number of financial publications are providing greater coverage of regional companies, companies with a specialized market niche or management, and companies that have recently gone public. When you read any of these publications, do so with an eye toward articles on OTC stocks.

Keeping Track of SEC Filings

The standard reference sources described in the foregoing section draw their information from company filings with the SEC. Figure 5–1 lists such filings together with descriptions of the information they contain. Of the filings listed, proxy statements and 13D filings are of particular significance to both individual and professional investors. A proxy statement contains a description of a company's management and principal shareholders (those holding 5% or more), and their ages and salaries (including direct and deferred compensation). Such background information about the principals in a corporation enables you to make judgments about the direction the company is taking and answers a number of important questions such as how important to a company's operation its outside directors are, whether its officers' salaries are higher or lower than industry norms, and whether the company is likely to be taken over—either on a friendly or hostile basis. By reading between the lines of a company's proxy statement you can find answers to these questions.

Likewise, 13D filings serve as a signal that a particular individual or institution plays a significant role in the affairs of a company, whether as an officer, director, or 5%

FIGURE 5–1.

S-1. The basic registration form, used to register offerings for which no other form is authorized or prescribed. Part I (the prospectus) contains, among other things:

- The name of the registrant, a brief description of the securities being offered, and the offering price and its determination
- Certain summary information, risk factors, and the ratio of earnings to fixed charges
- A description of the use of proceeds
- Information on any selling security holders
- A description of the securities being registered
- Any interests of named experts and counsel
- A description of registrant's business and property
- A description of material legal proceedings involving registrant
- Information on market prices and dividends on any common equity securities
- Financial statements
- Management's discussion and analysis of financial condition and results of operations
- Any disagreements with accountants on accounting and financial disclosure
- Information on registrant's directors and executive officers (including executive compensation)
- Information on the security ownership of management and certain beneficial owners

10-K. The annual report that most reporting companies file with the Commission each year. It provides a comprehensive overview of the registrant's state of business. The report must be filed within 90 days after the end of the company's fiscal year. The key items it contains are description of the business and of properties; legal proceedings; matters submitted to a vote of security holders; market for common equity and related shareholder matters; management's discussion and analysis of financial condition and results of operations; financial data and statements; disagreements on accounting and financial disclosure; list of directors and executive officers (including executive compensation); and security ownership of management and certain beneficial owners.

FIGURE 5–1 (cont'd.).

10-Q. A report filed quarterly by most registered companies. It includes unaudited financial statements and provides a continuing view of the company's financial position during the year. The report must be filed three times a year (the 10-K constitutes the fourth quarter report) and is due within 45 days of the close of each fiscal quarter. The report is in two parts. Part I contains financial statements and management's discussion and analysis of financial condition and results of operations. Part II contains other information such as legal proceedings, changes in securities, defaults upon senior securities, submission of matters to a vote of security holders, and any 8-K forms.

8-K. The "current report" used to report the occurrence of any material events or corporate changes of importance to investors or security holders. It provides more current information on certain specified events than would Forms 10-Q or 10-K.

- Changes in control of registrant
- Acquisition or disposition of assets
- Bankruptcy or receivership
- Changes in registrant's certifying accountant
- Other events—the registrant may, at its option, report under this item any events with respect to which information is not otherwise called for by this form, that the registrant deems of importance to investors
- Resignation of registrant's directors
- Financial statements, pro forma financial information, and exhibits

10. The general form used to register securities under the '34 Act. Among the items included are:

- Resignation of registrant's directors
- Financial statements and related information
- Certain security ownership information
- A list of directors and executive officers (including executive compensation)
- Discussion of any legal proceedings
- Market price of and dividends on the registrant's common equity
- Description of the securities to be registered
- Indemnification of directors and officers

FIGURE 5–1 (cont'd.).

- Any disagreements with accountants on accounting and financial disclosure

SCHEDULE 13D. Discloses beneficial ownership of certain registered equity securities. Any person or group of persons who acquire a beneficial ownership of more than 5% of a class of registered equity securities of certain issuers must file a Schedule 13D reporting such acquisition, together with certain other information, within 10 days after such acquisition. The schedule requires disclosure of the security and issuer; the identity and background of the reporting person; the source and amount of funds or other consideration for making the purchases; the purpose of the transaction; the extent of interest in securities of issuer; and contracts, arrangements, understandings, or relationships with respect to securities of issuer.

SCHEDULE 13G. This form, which is filed annually, is a much abbreviated version of Schedule 13D available only for use by a limited category of "persons" (such as banks, broker/dealers, and insurance companies) and then only when the securities were acquired in the ordinary course of business and not with the purpose nor effect of changing or influencing the control of the issuer.

3 and 4. Every director, officer, or owner of more than 10% of a class of equity securities registered under Section 12 of the '34 Act must file with the Commission a statement of ownership regarding such security. The initial filing is on Form 3, and changes are reported on Form 4. The forms contain information on the reporting person's relationship to the company and on his or her purchases and sales of such equity securities.

SCHEDULE 14D-1. Any person, other than the issuer itself (see Schedule 13E-4), making a tender offer for certain equity securities (such as equity securities registered pursuant to Section 12 of the '34 Act), which offer, if accepted, would cause that person to own over 5% of that class of the securities, must at the time of the offer file a Schedule 14D-1. It contains information about the securities being sought, such as title, amount, and price identity and background of bidder; past relationships between the bidder and the subject company; the source and amount of the funds or other consideration for the tender offer; the purpose of the tender offer and any plans or proposals of the bidder; any present interest of the bidder in the securities of the subject company; any connections between the bidder and any person with respect to any securities of the bidder; and financial statements of certain bidders.

SCHEDULE 14D-9. Must be filed with the Commission when an interested party, such as an issuer, a beneficial owner of securities, or a representative of either, makes a solicitation or recommendation to the shareholders with respect to a particular tender offer (a tender offer that is, of course, subject to Regulation 14D). Some of the elements of this schedule are the title of the class of equity securities; identification of the tender offer; identity and background of the person filing; and a discussion of the solicitation or recommendation, with the basis supporting the stated solicitation or recommendation.

PROSPECTUS

The prospectus constitutes Part I of 1933 Act registration statements. It contains the basic business and financial information about an issuer with respect to a particular securities offering. Investors may use the prospectus to help appraise the merits of the offering and make educated investment decisions. For further information see 1933 Act Registration Statements.

ANNUAL REPORT TO SHAREHOLDERS

The Annual Report to Shareholders is the principal document used by most public companies to disclose corporate information to shareholders. The Report is not a required SEC filing and, therefore, great discretion is left to the company as to what information will be included and how it will be presented. It is usually a state-of-the-company report including an opening letter from the Chief Executive Officer, financial data, results of continuing operations, market segment information, new product plans, subsidiary activities, and research and development activities on future programs.

PROXY AND PROXY SOLICITATION MATERIALS

A proxy statement is a document intended to provide security holders the information necessary to enable them to vote in an informed manner on matters to be brought up at security holders' meetings, whether the traditional annual meeting or a special meeting. Typically, a security holder is also provided with a "proxy" whereby he can authorize designated persons to vote his securities in the manner he wants in the event he himself does not attend the meeting. Definitive (final) copies of proxy statements and proxies are filed with the Commission at the time they are sent to security holders.

shareholder. A 13D filing (or a variation of it) must be made with the SEC by officers and directors of public companies, as well as by institutions or individuals who own 5% or more of a public company's common stock. The filing must be made within ten days of the acquisition of the 5% position. Also, any changes in such positions (increases or decreases) must be promptly reported to the SEC. Figure 5–2 is a sample of a 13D Form. The purpose of the 13D filing is to provide a level trading field—that is, to keep both small and large investors informed as to what so-called large, "sophisticated" investors are buying into. Many investors consider the filing of a 13D by a well-known market professional to be an indication that the stock is "in play" and that a takeover or restructuring is imminent.

To keep track of filings made with the SEC, you can read the *SEC News Digest,* which is published daily and lists all 13D filings and changes in position as they are received by the Commission. Further, the *SEC Monthly Summary of Insider Transactions* lists in alphabetical order all those companies that have seen purchases or sales of their stocks or bonds by officers, directors, or 5% shareholders. For a fee, you can subscribe to these publications by writing to the publications office of the SEC [Superintendent of Documents, Government Printing Office, Washington, D.C. 20402 / (202) 783-3238]; they are also available at most public libraries. Information about these filings is also reported in financial newspapers. The importance assigned to 13D filings is supported by the fact that a number of advisory services and investment newsletters have come into existence just to track such filings. The majority of these services are listed in Appendix I.

Because so many mergers, leveraged buyouts, and restructurings have occurred in recent years, you would do well to spend some time evaluating the importance of 13D filings. Obviously, the significance of a 13D filing varies from situation to situation, but certain guidelines generally apply. First, the weight you assign to any 13D filing is a function of the individual or entity making the filing.

The size of the position discussed in the 13D filing can be an indicator. Typically, a position of 5–10% indicates an initial interest on the part of the investor. On the other hand, such a small position may mean that the stock is difficult to acquire at all. An acquisition of a position of 5–10% usually means that the individual investor has time to look into the company and formulate an opinion. On the other hand, large initial position generally means that the stock is no longer undiscovered and, in fact, that the underlying assets of the particular company may be fully priced.

As you read the financial press, you will become familiar with the major M&A (merger and acquisitions) risk arbitrage (investing in proposed takeover company stocks), and LBO (leveraged buyout) firms. A filing of a 13D by any of these parties can signal you to look further into the company whose stock was bought. You might consult the standard reference sources such as S&P or Moodys, telephone the company to obtain an annual report and the most recent quarterly report, and apply the analytical tools in Appendix III to determine what the professional investor may have seen to warrant buying the stock.

As you become more familiar with the goals, methods, and techniques of particular "players," you will find it easier to project what is likely to follow the filing of a 13D. Is this particular investor an "asset player"—that is, someone who buys into companies selling at a discount from their true value and once in control liquidates the company? Or is this investor someone who actively and successfully acquires companies and then merges the acquired companies into an existing business? Or is the filer of the 13D a "greenmailer," that is, someone who seeks to get the particular company to buy out the position at a price above the original purchase price? As you become more familiar with the various players, you learn to gauge their objectives and determine whether the 13D filer's objectives fit your own goals and attitudes towards risk.

How to Use Personal Contacts

For Investment Ideas. To this point, the approaches to investing you have learned rely on your ability to locate and

FIGURE 5–2. Sample of a 13D Form.

OMB APPROVAL
OMB Number: 3235-0145 Expires: September 30, 1988

SECURITIES AND EXCHANGE COMMISSION
Washington, D.C. 20549

SCHEDULE 13D

Under the Securities Exchange Act of 1934
(Amendment No. ________)*

____
(Name of Issuer)

____
(Title of Class of Securities)

____
(CUSIP Number)

____
(Name, Address and Telephone Number of Person Authorized to Receive Notices and Communications)

____
(Date of Event which Requires Filing of this Statement)

If the filing person has previously filed a statement on Schedule 13G to report the acquisition which is the subject of this Schedule 13D, and is filing this schedule because of Rule 13d-1(b)(3) or (4), check the following box ☐.

Check the following box if a fee is being paid with the statement ☐. (A fee is not required only if the reporting person: (1) has a previous statement on file reporting beneficial ownership of more than five percent of the class of securities described in Item 1; and (2) has filed no amendment subsequent thereto reporting beneficial ownership of five percent or less of such class.) (See Rule 13d-7.)

Note: Six copies of this statement, including all exhibits, should be filed with the Commission. See Rule 13d-1(a) for other parties to whom copies are to be sent.

*The remainder of this cover page shall be filled out for a reporting person's initial filing on this form with respect to the subject class of securities, and for any subsequent amendment containing information which would alter disclosures provided in a prior cover page.

The information required on the remainder of this cover page shall not be deemed to be "filed" for the purpose of Section 18 of the Securities Exchange Act of 1934 ("Act") or otherwise subject to the liabilities of that section of the Act but shall be subject to all other provisions of the Act (however, see the Notes).

SEC 1746 (10-87)

FIGURE 5–2. Sample of a 13D Form (cont'd.).

SCHEDULE 13D

CUSIP No. ____________ Page ______ of ______ Pages

1	NAME OF REPORTING PERSON S.S. OR I.R.S. IDENTIFICATION NO. OF ABOVE PERSON
2	CHECK THE APPROPRIATE BOX IF A MEMBER OF A GROUP* (a) ☐ (b) ☐
3	SEC USE ONLY
4	SOURCE OF FUNDS*
5	CHECK BOX IF DISCLOSURE OF LEGAL PROCEEDINGS IS REQUIRED PURSUANT TO ITEMS 2(d) or 2(E) ☐
6	CITIZENSHIP OR PLACE OF ORGANIZATION

NUMBER OF SHARES BENEFICIALLY OWNED BY EACH REPORTING PERSON WITH		
	7	SOLE VOTING POWER
	8	SHARED VOTING POWER
	9	SOLE DISPOSITIVE POWER
	10	SHARED DISPOSITIVE POWER

11	AGGREGATE AMOUNT BENEFICIALLY OWNED BY EACH REPORTING PERSON
12	CHECK BOX IF THE AGGREGATE AMOUNT IN ROW (11) EXCLUDES CERTAIN SHARES* ☐
13	PERCENT OF CLASS REPRESENTED BY AMOUNT IN ROW (11)
14	TYPE OF REPORTING PERSON*

*SEE INSTRUCTIONS BEFORE FILLING OUT!

SEC 1746 (10-87) 2 of 7

analyze factual data. But as a successful investor, you also need to deal with people. The following paragraphs introduce you to the "tricks" for turning people—friends, business associates, social acquaintances, or corporate management—into worthwhile sources of investment ideas and information.

You can start by turning your job or profession into a source of investment ideas. For example, let's assume you are a teacher by profession. Your day-to-day work in the classroom makes you familiar with many of the newest and most effective learning tools. Because you have this expertise, you may be particularly impressed with some new product offered by a small-cap, learning-products company traded over the counter. Investing in such a company before it is discovered by market professionals could prove extremely profitable.

Similarly, as a consumer you encounter goods and services that you consider to be well above the norm. If you like a particular product, go one step further and determine if its manufacturer or supplier is a publicly traded company. You may just find that—like its products or services—the company's financials are attractive. In just this manner you may identify an undervalued stock among the many categories of OTC stocks described in the foregoing chapters of this book.

In the case of regional companies, the significance of personal contacts deserves additional attention: Personal contacts may be the only way to locate such investment situations. Beyond the community or region where the company is located, few investors may even be aware of the company's existence or of the fact that its shares are publicly traded. By keeping alert to the existence and activities of the companies located in your particular community or region, you may discover a surprising number of inefficiently priced stocks. Investing in a company before it gains national recognition can enable you to reap substantial profits on a small initial investment.

For Evaluating Management. Many individuals hesitate to pick up the telephone or write to a corporation's management to request information or to ask a question. This hesitancy is only natural, but after the first time you will find the task easy. Requesting a copy of the company's annual report, 10K, proxy statement, and 10Q—the documents typically requested—by telephone or by letter is the best way to initiate contact with a company you are considering investing in. With few exceptions, companies are only too happy to supply such documents to individual investors. After all, a company benefits by fostering interest in itself and its "story." (In the rare event that you receive an unfriendly or hostile response to your request, look elsewhere for investment opportunities.) On the other hand, be wary of investing in a company whose management appears to be more knowledgeable about the price of its stock than about the company's ongoing business.

Once you have received the information requested, scan it quickly. Most companies do not survive this initial review of their financials. Next, apply the appropriate number crunching techniques (discussed in Chapters 3 and 4 and described in detail in Appendix III) to further narrow down your search. If you review a hundred annual reports you will likely find twenty-five or fewer companies that warrant personal contact. As you go through this scanning/number crunching process, you will turn up questions that can be answered only by the company's management. Many professional investors make it a practice not to purchase a single share of a company's stock without speaking to or meeting with the company's management personally; individual investors could prevent a lot of bad investments by adopting the same rule.

A typical concern is whom to speak to when contacting a company's management. Obviously, addressing the highest possible level of management is best, but it is not always possible to contact a company's chief executive officer or financial officer. In some cases, you may find that senior management is eager to talk to you; in other cases the call may be shifted to someone in the finance or public relations department. Remember that, while it is desirable to speak to senior management, your objective is to make the initial contact with the company's management—at whatever level. If your scanning and number crunching convince you that the company is worth investing in, you can call the company for updates on its progress and in that way cement and build on the relationship you started with your initial contact. Also, number crunching may help you formulate some intelligent questions to pose to management. The following lists some of the kinds of questions you might wish to ask.

1. After reviewing the reports you sent me, I see that the company's sales have shown a continuing pattern of growth. How do you account for this pattern and do you see it continuing in the future?
2. Earnings have been growing at a rapid rate. Do you see this trend continuing in the future? Has the company been able to maintain and/or expand its profit margin as its sales have grown? Is the company's product mix shifting toward higher-profit-margin products?
3. Is the company presently involved in or contemplating in the near future modernizing or expanding its plant capacity?
4. How will the company finance plant expansion or modernization (for example, with debt or with internally generated funds)?
5. The company is selling at a relatively low price-earnings ratio. Do you have any feelings about why this is so? Do you see any reason why this should change in the future?
6. Aside from what was described in the annual report, quarterly reports, and so forth that you sent me, has the company developed any new products, expanded into new markets, or undergone restructuring of corporate assets?
7. Have any other individual or institutional analysts contacted you recently? If so, do you know whether they have written research reports about the company and whether I can obtain copies of such reports?

The foregoing questions are geared principally to growth situations. The following questions are directed toward companies representing asset-rich, rather than growth situations.

8. What is the reason for the substantial amount of cash, short-term investments, or marketable securities reflected on the company's balance sheet? What plans does the company have for utilizing its large cash horde in the business or for distributing it to shareholders?
9. What is the nature of the company's real estate holdings (undeveloped land, developed land, or leases)? Does the company plan to sell, develop, or lease its real estate holdings? (The liquidation of some parts of the business to realize the cash needed for development or, alternatively, the hiring of planners or developers may signal that the company is planning to develop its real estate holdings.)
10. Has the company adopted any "poison-pill" provisions, changed its state of incorporation and/or corporate charter, or initiated a stock repurchase program? If not, does the company contemplate these or similar moves?

Undoubtedly, this list is far from complete. The particular questions you will want to ask are influenced by such factors as the nature of the company's business, its management style, and the perception and knowledge you yourself bring to the questioning process. Bear in mind that you are seeking to establish and cultivate personal contact with company's management. Give weight to the *way* management does or does not answer your questions, as well as to any impressions you may get about management's strengths or weaknesses. As any experienced investor will tell you, invest only in those companies whose managements you respect and believe in.

Whenever possible, attend the annual meeting of any company you are thinking of investing in heavily or have already made a substantial investment in. By attending the company's annual meeting you find out who the real forces in the company are and what family or business relationships exist within the management structure. On paper, the company's financials may appear impressive and you might believe that the company represents an undiscovered situation. But once you attend an annual meeting and meet the company's management face to face you may come to understand why the company's stock is selling at such a cheap price. You may find that management is too rigid, that the company is run solely for the benefit of management with little concern for the shareholders, or that the company's management has little interest in publicizing the company's story. Management may be weak or shallow—characteristics you could not have perceived by simply looking at the numbers.

On the other hand, you may come away from the meeting with a favorable impression. In either case, when you leave the annual meeting, you will probably have reached a conclusion as to whether to buy, sell, or hold the company's stock.

IF YOU INVEST WITH THE PROS ...

For a variety of reasons, many individuals are not interested in making direct investments in over-the-counter stocks. They prefer to turn the task over to market professionals. If this is your choice, you are still left with the task of selecting an investment advisor who specializes in OTC stocks or a mutual fund whose portfolio consists of such issues.

Choosing an Investment Advisor

If you decide to select an investment advisor, you should follow certain general rules. First, ask any advisor you are considering retaining for information about his or her track record or performance history. Second, confirm that the advisor is registered with the appropriate federal and state authorities and has a clean record with such authorities. Third, be sure that you are comfortable with the advisor: The advisor's approach to investing should match your own and both of you should agree on the level of risk and the amount of assets to be committed to the OTC marketplace. (As was true in selecting a broker, the best way of locating a suitable advisor is probably through the recommendation of friends and business associates.)

Mutual Funds

Alternatively, you may decide—as do many investors—to invest in the over-the-counter market via a mutual fund. Indeed, a number of professional investors manage funds with holdings concentrated in OTC stocks. For this reason, selecting a single fund or even a group of funds that would satisfy every investor's needs or goals is impossible. Therefore, the emphasis here is on identifying the way mutual funds select individual over-the-counter stocks. Three different funds, along with their different investment philosophies, are explored in this section of the book.

The Over-the-Counter Fund, Inc. Founded by Ralph P. Coleman, Jr. in 1955, the Over-the-Counter is the original fund investing principally in OTC securities. The Over-the-Counter Fund, Inc. is an open-end, diversified, management company offering investors the opportunity to own a professionally managed portfolio of over-the-counter securities selected for long-term growth of capital. The fund's May 1, 1988 prospectus points out that there are currently more than 5700 issues eligible for trading in the OTC market. Over the past ten years, NASDAQ share volume has grown over 1800%—three times faster than any other United States stock market—making the OTC market the third largest in the world, following the Tokyo Exchange and the New York Stock Exchange. Page 7 of the fund's prospectus describes its investment philosophy as follows:

"The Fund is designed for long-term investors who have the perspective, patience and financial ability to accept greater investment risks in search of substantial long-term rewards. Companies whose securities trade on the OTC market are generally smaller or newer than those listed on exchanges, and may have limited product lines or relatively new products or services, may lack established markets, depth of experienced management or the ability to generate funds. The securities of these companies may have more limited marketability and may be subject to greater price volatility than securities of larger companies. However, companies in which the Fund invests may offer greater opportunities for capital appreciation than larger, more established companies. In addition, since the securities of many of these smaller companies may be overlooked by the investment community and, therefore, may be undervalued, there exists the potential for significant capital appreciation."

In terms of how the fund goes about identifying appropriate OTC stocks, page 4 of the Semiannual Report of the Over-the-Counter Fund for the six months ended June 30, 1987 describes the fund's criteria and standards for selecting appropriate stocks:

"Our definition of value is an eclectic one, and our research leads us to identify four very different kinds of opportunities. 1) The classic price/earnings approach where we buy companies whose stock prices fail to reflect growth prospects. This produces a low-P/E bias in this portfolio, but by no means rules out rapidly growing companies. 2) The asset value approach, where we can buy companies at a healthy discount to their liquidation value. It helps when the companies involved are actively exploiting those assets, as is often the case with real estate developers, but we will buy stagnating assets as well if the price is cheap enough. 3) Buying the business at a value price. We examine companies as a businessman would, looking for cash flow, a market niche or franchise, or the restructuring potential of improving management or terminating losing operations. 4) Buying participations in industries where we firmly believe consensus opinion is wrong, such as the savings and loan industry at present, or in sectors of the economy which have been overlooked, such as high-service trucking or original equipment auto part suppliers."

The foregoing statement of the Over-the-Counter Fund's philosophy and approach to investing is reflected in the fund's performance over an extended period of time. However, past performance does not guarantee future performance. For additional information about this fund you can call 1-800-523-2578 or write to the fund at State Street Bank & Trust Company, National Financial Data Services, P.O. Box 26070, Kansas City, Mo. 64196-6070.

Herzog, Heine Geduld, Inc.—Mutual Shares Corporation et. al. Another family of funds with a heavy orientation toward over-the-counter stocks is the Mutual Shares Corporation Fund Group. Mutual Shares' management avoids the so-called Nifty Fifty (well-known companies heavily owned by institutions) and concentrates on "bottom fishing." This fund's approach to investing calls for reviewing bankruptcy filings; following the activities of regional companies, which typically are closely held and thinly traded; and continually looking out for companies with substantial current assets, hidden assets, or valuable business franchises. Investing in any one of the funds managed by Mutual Shares enables you to invest in two of the principal categories of OTC stocks described in Chapters 3 and 4, that is, bankrupt companies and companies being restructured or liquidated, and regional companies.

Again, as with the Over-the-Counter Fund, it is essential that you personally examine the fund's prospectus and evaluate its track record before you invest in it. To obtain copies of Mutual Shares' prospectus call 1-800-457-0211 or write to the fund at 26 Broadway, New York, N.Y. 10004.

Charles Royce—Royce Value and Pennsylvania Mutual Fund. A third portfolio manager who directs attention to the OTC marketplace in particular is Charles Royce. Royce advocates investing in small-capitalization companies, which are principally traded over the counter. As a value-oriented investor, he prefers to invest for the long term rather than chase each year's fad stocks. Also, he likes smaller companies because he believes that over time they have greater opportunities to grow and thus promise higher returns.

What techniques does Royce use to identify suitable OTC stocks? For the most part, he relies on the same techniques described in this book; namely, the application of numerical ratios to identify asset-rich companies. Royce adds one caveat to this: He is willing to pay more for assets that generate sustainable high returns.

Before you invest in this fund, read the prospectus thoroughly. A copy of Royce Value Fund's Prospectus can be obtained by calling either 1-800-221-4268 or (212) 355-7311 or by writing the fund at Royce Value Fund, 1414 Avenue of the Americas, New York, N.Y. 10019.

The information in these five chapters includes all the basic principles you need to understand in order to be able to invest intelligently in the over-the-counter market. The last chapter is intended to bring you up-to-date on developments in the OTC market since the October 19, 1987 market break.

6

The OTC Marketplace: Life After October 19

The market break of October 19, 1987 has had a significant impact on the investment world, and the over-the-counter marketplace is no exception. This impact is expressed not just in dollars and cents, but in the way business is conducted, in investor sentiment, and in changes to the rules and regulations governing OTC trading that have been implemented since that memorable October day.

WHAT HAPPENED?

The facts are as follows: On October 19, 1987, the Dow Jones Industrial Average plunged 508 points or 22.6% in a single session and a total of 604 million shares changed hands on the floor of the New York Stock Exchange. On that same day, the Nikkei index plummeted 14.9% (a record 3,836 points) on a low volume of approximately 500 million shares. The Nikkei index ended the week at 21,910—well below the preceding weeks' high of 26,000. The London Stock Exchange closed at 1403.5—some 400 points below its average of 1800 just 13 days before. In addition, the OTC Composite Index declined to 360.21 on October 19, 1987 from a high of 406.33 on October 18, 1987, for a better than 11% decline in a single day.

Almost immediately after "Black Monday," studies were undertaken to determine the causes for the market's sudden fall. Much of the "blame" has been principally attributed to such institutional activities as program and index fund trading and portfolio insurance activities. Furthermore, some of the blame for the October 19 "happening" is attributed to the activities of foreign investors as well as such mundane acts as the ability of today's investors—via telephone switching—to move money instantaneously from a stock fund to a bond or money market fund (a safer haven) within the same family of funds. Overriding one single cause is the fact that on Monday, October 19, the majority of the investment world's mega-chip players decided to cash in and turned a minor decline into a record-breaking market crash.

On the NYSE, 15% or more of the volume on Black Monday came from *program trading*—best described as computer-activated programs to automatically buy or sell stock based on prior directions given to the computer. In a typical scenario, a trader utilizes a computer program to monitor a "basket" of stocks modeled after the stocks contained in a popular market index such as the S&P 100. At the same time the trader tracks the stock index, which is traded as a futures commodity on the Chicago Mercantile Exchange. When the stock market experiences a substantial movement up or down, the futures contract typically reacts less slowly than the stock market. Institutional and professional investors use computers to take advantage of this temporary difference or spread between the two markets by making almost instantaneous transactions. Program trading works with the help of the Designated Order Turnaround (DOT) system instituted a few years ago by the New York Stock Exchange. This system allows institutional investors to direct their orders to the specialist on the floor of the exchange instantaneously—without having to go through a broker. By eliminating the human element that requires time to think and function, program traders can capitalize on any differences between marketplaces no matter how small or how short-lived the spreads.

Portfolio insurance, also cited as a principal factor behind Black Monday, is an outgrowth of program trading although it appeared on the investment scene only in recent years. On October 19, approximately $80 billion worth of portfolios were insured—up from $40 billion at the end of 1986 and $4 billion a year earlier. Much of the program trading that took place on October 19 was related to portfolio insurance.

How did these activities affect the market on Black Monday? In theory, when the stock market begins to decline, the program trader comes in and sells stock index futures. If the market reverses itself and begins to rise the trader will lose on the futures contracts, but that loss should be offset by the increase in the value of the stocks still held. On the other hand, if the market continues to fall, the decline in the value of the stocks held will be cushioned by the increasing value of the futures position. If the market continued to fall, more future contracts would be sold. Both portfolio insurance and program trading assume that it will always be possible to execute transactions on both the exchange and the futures market and that the transaction costs associated with futures contracts will be less than with stock transactions. Thus, the goal of portfolio insurance is to protect the worth of an existing portfolio by hedging it with offsetting index options, whereas program trading seeks to profit by exploiting differences between two markets—the Dow Jones Industrial Average (or basket of stocks) versus index options.

The concepts of program trading and portfolio insurance rest on the assumption of continuous markets, and this belief was put to a severe test on Monday, October 19, 1987. Over the preceding weekend, investors had had the opportunity to assess the previous week's drop of 235 points in the Dow Jones Industrial Average. Some investors probably concluded that there was virtue in being cautious, particularly in light of the fact that such traditional investment measures as price-earnings ratios and dividend yields pointed to danger ahead. These factors, combined with certain negative political and economic developments (such as the number of scandals surrounding the Reagan administration and concern over U.S. balance of payment deficits and fears of renewed inflation), sent the DJIA down by more than 200 points as the first wave of selling hit the marketplace. The portfolio insurers figured heavily in this selling as they liquidated both stocks and futures contracts. In this market freefall, no buyers were available at any price and specialists were required to take in large amounts of stock. However, the program traders and portfolio insurers did not escape unscathed from the rapid market decline. On Tuesday, October 20, many of these institutional traders found that the unthought of had happened—the market closed down. One by one the large capitalization stocks halted trading, with no bids and hundreds of thousands of shares offered by panicked sellers. With the majority of large-cap stocks not trading, stock index futures traders had no idea how to price the futures contracts and the futures markets closed down. Only when a number of major brokerage firms stepped into the breach with bids for many of these big-cap stocks did the market stabilize. The lesson to be learned from all this is that the sophisticated systems and programs available to today's investor do not replace common sense and that such systems have not eliminated fluctuations and market cycles.

HOW OTC EXECUTION HAS CHANGED SINCE OCTOBER 19

The decline in the OTC market was on the order of what the exchanges experienced—20% or more. A number of "war stories" are told about the difficulty of getting through to market makers—when it was possible at all—and about the difficult of getting trades executed. Many retail and institutional customers were unable to reach their registered representatives or mutual funds on Black Monday. The following example highlights what happened to a typical trader who did reach a market maker that day. John Trader told of getting through to a market maker and indicating that he planned to "hit" (to sell) 1000 shares at the bid price shown by the market maker on the NASDAQ screen. The market maker responded by saying that the quote was in error and the bid was, in fact, lower. When the trader accepted the lower bid, he was told that it was good for only 100 shares—the amount that a market maker is required to buy or sell under the NASD rules in effect at that time.

Many traders were unable to execute transactions because, at least in some instances, market makers had ceased to perform their function. Indeed, the allegation was made that some market makers "walked away from the market" and failed even to answer their phones. The market makers were able to act in this way because the NASD rules in effect at that time did not require them to maintain an orderly and efficient market, as do exchange rules for specialists. The NASD rules in effect on October 19 were not as stringent as those enacted by the various exchanges to regulate the activities of specialists—those individuals and firms who perform many of the same functions as those of market makers in the OTC market. But, almost immediately after October 19, and on a continuing basis, efforts were undertaken to improve the effectiveness and responsiveness of the market maker system. These improvements will be described shortly.

At this point, it would be appropriate to describe two problems peculiar to the over-the-counter marketplace which were brought to light by the events of October 19. These are locked trades and crossed trades. Both such trades have the effect of freezing or preventing the market makers from performing their function at a time—a sharp market decline—when they are most needed. A locked trade occurs when a market maker inadvertently offers to buy a stock at the same price at which another market maker is willing to sell it. A crossed trade takes place when one dealer offers to buy a stock for more than another is willing to sell it for. These market irregularities between buy and sell prices typically occur during hectic trading times when market makers do not have enough time to adjust their quotes to changing conditions.

Figure 6–1 describes a series of rules adopted by the NASD (with SEC approval) to solve the problems brought to light by the events of October 19 and 20. These new trading rules have two objectives—stabilizing prices for large orders and encouraging market makers to continue to function whatever the market conditions. These new rules should make the OTC market a more attractive arena for trading or investing.

The first rule is designed to discourage market makers from dropping out of the NASDAQ system when markets turn against them. Market makers are now required to keep posting prices on the system, and a market maker who withdraws from making a market in a particular stock is barred from dealing in that issue for 20 business days.

The second rule makes participation in the Automated Trading System mandatory, whereas in the past membership was optional. The Automated Trading System involves the concept of trades being executed without human participation beyond the original placing of the order in the buyer's computer terminal. As noted in Figure 6–1, only 210 of 540 market makers presently participate in the system, so Rule #2 would add additional depth to the system. Approximately 13% of all NASD transactions are currently executed through the Small Order Execution System (SOES)—a computer activated rather than a voice-contact system—and it is anticipated that with the implementation of Rule #2 this figure would jump to between 25 and 30%. This rule also provides for execution through SOES of orders up to 1000 shares on 3000 NASD stocks and up to 500 shares on the remaining 2700 NASD securities.

The remaining two rules address other "glitches" that surfaced during the hectic days of October 19 and 20. Rule #3 provides that the automated trading system would be called in to execute so-called locked and cross trades. The purpose of this is to unfreeze the market maker function and prevent the market from, in effect, closing down.

Rule #4 calls for the implementation of a SOES limit-order function which enables subscribers, that is, small investors, to enter limit orders that are reasonably related to

FIGURE 6–1.

NASD

FOR IMMEDIATE RELEASE
January 21, 1988

CONTACT: Enno Hobbing
(202) 728-8055
Jim Anderson
(212) 557-0100

NASD BOARD APPROVES SMALL ORDER EXECUTION SYSTEM ENHANCEMENTS

SOES Limit-Order File and OTC Bulletin Board Get Go Ahead

Washington, D.C.—The Board of Governors of the National Association of Securities Dealers, Inc. (NASD), at its meeting this week approved a series of enhancements to strengthen its Small Order Execution System (SOES) for the NASDAQ market. SOES provides automatic, computer-to-computer execution of investors' orders in NASDAQ securities.

The Board proposed the SOES enhancements to the NASD membership and to NASDAQ companies in November. They are designed to improve computer access to the NASDAQ market and to strengthen the commitment of market makers. Some 46 comment letters were received on the proposals and taken into account in this week's decisions by the Board.

"Individual investors are the principal force in the NASDAQ market," NASD President Joseph R. Hardiman said. "These improvements to SOES will make it much more accessible and useful to them, especially in fast moving, volatile markets."

The SOES enhancements, which will soon be filed with the SEC for approval, do the following:

- Create new, affirmative, competitive incentives for market makers to make continuous markets by prohibiting, for 20 business days, the resumption of market making in an issue by a firm that

FIGURE 6–1 (cont'd.).

withdraws as market maker for reasons other than those permitted under a narrowly defined excused withdrawal provision. Although the acceptable reasons for an excused withdrawal from market making will be limited, the rules will provide for appropriate rights of appeal for any request denied.

- Make participation in the system mandatory for all market makers in NASDAQ/NMS securities. Participation is currently optional, and 210 of our 540 market makers use the system. This change should substantially increase the number of transactions executed automatically by SOES from the present 13% to as much as 25–30%.
- Provide for different maximum order size limits that take into account the characteristics of different securities. Presently, the order size limits are 1,000 shares for NASDAQ/NMS securities and 500 shares for other NASDAQ securities.
- Continue SOES operations in instances in which quotations are locked or crossed. (When a market maker enters an offer price that is equal to another market maker's best bid price in the same security, the market is said to be locked; when an offer is less than another's best bid, the market is said to be crossed. Locked and crossed quotations also occur when market makers enter bid prices that are equal to or greater than the offer price of another market maker in the same security. Presently SOES will not execute orders in a security when quotations are locked or crossed.) Under the new rules, SOES will execute against the market maker causing the locked or crossed market, if that secures the best price for the customer. In addition to giving investors continuous access to SOES under all market conditions, this change will also give market makers an economic incentive to keep their quotations current.

"We expect early SEC approval for these improvements to SOES," Mr. Hardiman said. "Together with the approval which the Commission gave last week to our Order Confirmation Transaction (OCT) enhancement, our new system services can drastically reduce the use of the telephone, and greatly increase the ease and speed of NASDAQ trading."

FIGURE 6–1 (cont'd.).

SOES Limit-Order File Enhancement

In a related action, the NASD Board determined to move forward and implement a SOES limit-order file capability, currently under development, immediately following the introduction of the rules and enhancements required for a mandatory SOES.

This SOES enhancement will enable subscribers to enter limit order for their customers that are reasonably related to the market, with the understanding that if an order cannot be executed immediately, it would be held in SOES until the limit price was reached. When the best bid/ask changes so that it is equal to or better than the limit price, the system would seek to execute the order against SOES market makers. Limit orders will be given precedence over market orders, based on time of entry, for executions at a given price and the file will accept "good 'til date" orders.

New OTC Bulletin Board

The Board also approved the development of a new information system designated the OTC Bulletin Board Service. The service will permit subscribers to access information entered by market makers in non-NASDAQ securities. Through this system, participants will be able to enter and advertise, by security, their telephone numbers, quotations—which, unlike NASDAQ, need not be firm—and other pertinent information on non-NASDAQ securities.

This new information service, coupled with an NASD proposal recently filed with the SEC to require members to electronically report daily price and volume information on trades in non-NASDAQ securities, will upgrade the quality of information available for securities that trade in this market and improve the ability of the NASD to regulate and surveil activity in it.

---

the market. An order that cannot be executed immediately would be held in the SOES system until the limit price is reached. Thus, the small investor has some of the same protections available to the investor in exchange-listed stocks.

Also in response to the problems that surfaced on Black Monday, the NASD implemented a new computerized system that, over the next few years, will eliminate the use of telephones for trading in blocks of more than 1000 shares. Large orders are received directly on the terminals of the market-making firms and are accepted or rejected merely by pressing a button. This system should go a long way toward solving the problem that institutions and individual investors faced when trying to get through to market makers—finding that jammed phone lines prevented them from conducting their business.

HOW THE MARKET BREAK AFFECTED DIFFERENT TYPES OF OTC STOCKS

Not all over-the-counter stocks were impacted to the same degree or in the same manner by the events of October 19. Because the types of stocks traded over the counter are so different (as discussed in Chapters 3 and 4), the various categories reacted differently to the market break and some categories of OTC stocks have recovered more of their market value than others.

First let's consider how OTC blue chips reacted on Black Monday. Because many of these stocks are held principally by institutional investors as opposed to individual investors (they can be characterized as the OTC equivalent of the Dow Jones Average "basket of stocks"), they tracked the almost 23% drop in the DJIA. As with many listed big-cap stocks, many OTC blue chip stocks dropped sharply. In many cases it was difficult or impossible to reach market makers and some of them walked away from the market when contacted. However, as with listed big-cap stocks, when the OTC market stabilized, the majority of these stocks recovered a substantial portion of the price loss they suffered on October 19 and 20.

Second, let's examine what occurred in the case of bank, insurance company, and savings and loan stocks and the stocks of smokestack America. Although these stocks did decline, a surprising number of them fared much better than many exchange-listed stocks. The reason for this related to the nature of the principal shareholders of such companies. Many of the principal shareholders of financial institutions and regional companies are individual investors as opposed to institutions. Also, in the case of many such stocks, control (that is, ownership of 50% or more of the company's common stock) rests in the hands of only a few individuals. Because these individuals control so much of their company's stocks, they tended to react in two ways on Black Monday. On the one hand, they acted as a stabilizing force by holding on to their positions because they viewed their companies as operating entities and not merely as stocks to be bought or sold. Also, they knew full well how difficult it would be to liquidate a large position during a market break. Alternatively, they reacted positively by buying in their company's stocks either through a publicly announced repurchase program or through individual investments. For these reasons, the stocks of financial companies and regional companies declined the least and staged some of the strongest recoveries from their October lows.

New issue stocks present a different situation. Here the market corrected many abuses that had arisen over the past few years. As a result, new issues, particularly those of "concept" or start-up companies, dropped dramatically in price—losing as much as 80% or more of their value. Many of these "concept" new issues completely stopped trading as market makers liquidated their positions and have not recovered from the effects of the market break. On the other hand, although the majority of substantial new issues—those new issues with earnings and assets behind them—dropped sharply in price (20% or more) on October 19 and 20, they have for the most part recovered nearly all their lost value.

Penny stocks were perhaps the biggest losers in the market break and for the most part have failed to recover. Historically both penny stocks and new issues are the last categories of OTC stocks investors turn their attention to, and are most severely—sometimes fatally—affected by a sharp market downturn.

On Black Monday, foreign stocks reacted to two forces. On the one hand, many of these stocks dropped sharply in response to the decline occurring overseas. The Japanese market was especially impacted because of the relatively high price-earnings ratios of the stocks before October 19. European markets were generally less affected. At the same time, foreign stocks were buffeted by the selling occurring in the American OTC marketplace. Many foreign stocks trading over the counter suffered declines of 20% or more. Since then, many of these stocks have recovered the value lost in October, as American and overseas markets stabilized and moved upward.

Bankrupt stocks were impacted to a lesser degree than other OTC stocks during the market break. Because these stocks are viewed as "special situations" followed by institutional and individual investors with the expertise to analyze them, what selling pressure occurred on October 19 and 20 came from institutional and individual investors who needed funds to meet commitments in other parts of the marketplace. As with most other categories of OTC stocks, bankrupt stocks have recovered much of their lost value.

THE FUTURE OF OTC INVESTING

As a final note, some general observations can be made about how the over-the-counter market has fared since October 19, 1987. First, while rumors abound about big-cap stocks currently "in play," (that is, subject to impending takeover or restructuring), *secondary stocks*—defined as those whose total market value is less than $500 million, and which are principally traded over the counter—have performed better since the market break than the majority of the big-cap stocks.

Several factors lie behind this pattern. First, a number of major analysts and portfolio managers have advised their clients that secondary stocks appear "historically cheap" largely because investor interest has centered on the takeover stocks and mutual funds concentrating their holdings in such stocks. As a result of this lack of interest in secondary stocks "inefficiencies" have developed, and in many instances the market prices of secondary stocks do not reflect their true worth. Reacting to this situation, pension plans, mutual funds, and individual investors have committed more of their assets to the over-the-counter marketplace and such stocks have appreciated in price.

Will this pattern continue in the future? If history is any guide, markets go through cycles and fads: No market segment goes straight up. However, a number of recent studies have concluded that over an extended period of time—twenty years or more—the secondary, small-cap stocks have outperformed the large big-cap stocks. A principal reason given for this pattern is that small-cap stocks, because of their small size and generally unbureaucratic approach to doing business, offer better growth opportunities. In many instances small-cap stocks, particularly financial companies, regional companies, and some substantial new issues, sell at low price-to-earnings ratios and low P/E stocks have historically performed better than high P/E stocks.

In many respects, the over-the-counter market represents the last frontier for the individual investor. In this marketplace, the individual investor has distinct advantages over the institutional investor. Because of its fragmented nature, by utilizing the tools and techniques described in this book, the individual investor should be able to identify a number of undervalued asset plays or unrecognized growth stocks before they become discovered by market professionals. Investing in the over-the-counter market enables one to participate in the early and rapid growth stage of a company's development in the case of a growth stock or to buy assets at a discount before such asset plays are uncovered by market professionals, who typically focus most of their efforts on listed stocks.

While this book has furnished an overview of the whole over-the-counter market, another book published by the New York Institute of Finance entitled *Asset Plays* deals specifically with the valuation of asset-rich companies, and would be useful reading for the individual investor.

APPENDIX I

Investment Publications Particularly Relevant to the Over-the-Counter Market

GROWTH STOCK OUTLOOK AND JUNIOR GROWTH STOCKS

Published by Growth Stock Outlook
P.O. Box 9911
Chevy Chase, MD 20815
Twice Monthly ($95 per year)

These publications contain descriptions and frequent updates on rapid growth companies, the majority of which are traded over the counter. Charles Allmon, editor and publisher of *Growth Stock Outlook,* has followed such companies for more than twenty years and is the advisor to the Growth Stock Fund, a recently established closed-end fund.

THE INSIDER CHRONICLE

Published by Capitol Publications, Inc.
1300N 17th Street
Arlington, VA 22209
Weekly ($325 per year)

This publication draws from and analyzes the 130 filings made with the SEC by corporate officers, financial institutions, and merger and acquisition "players." Many such filings concern OTC stocks.

THE UNLISTED MARKET GUIDE

Published by The Unlisted Market Guide
P.O. Box 106
30 Glen Head Road
Glen Head, NY 11545
A bound service ($195 per year)

This guide provides reports on 250+ obscure over-the-counter companies which are not actively followed even by OTC professionals. A useful source of information on regional, thinly traded companies as well as some low-priced issues overlooked by the marketplace.

THE BOWSER REPORT

Published by The Bowser Report
P.O. Box 6278
Newport News, VA 23606-06278
Monthly ($36 per year)

This service seeks to provide a detailed approach to investing in stocks selling at $3 or less. Monthly recommendations are made and individual brokers are recommended.

THE INSIDERS

Published by The Insiders
3471 North Federal Highway
Fort Lauderdale, FL 33306
Monthly ($49 per year)

This publication furnishes the reader with information as to 13D filings as well as to the publisher's opinion as to the significance of the filing. This is perhaps the first publication that provided such information and used it as the focus of its investment philosophy.

THE RHM SURVEY OF WARRANTS, OPTIONS AND LOW-PRICED STOCKS

Published by RHM Associates
172 Forest Avenue
Glen Cove, NY 11542
Weekly ($130 per year)

This survey seeks to alert its readers to low-priced stocks (typically OTC) offering high profit potential. It also spotlights warrants and options that offer high potential.

CHAPTER II REPORTER

Published by Business Laws, Inc.
8228 Mayfield Road
Chesterland, OH 44026
Monthly ($78.50 per year)

This monthly newsletter is directed to professionals involved in business turnarounds, workouts, and Chapter II reorganizations. A useful tool for the individual and professional investor looking for "ideas" and "possible investments" in this area of the OTC marketplace.

THE WEEKLY TAKEOVER TARGET FORECAST

Published by Quality Services Company
5290 Overpass Road
Santa Barbara, CA 93111
Weekly ($195 per year)

This forecast highlights potential takeover targets traded on exchanges as well as over the counter and follows up on prior recommendations.

MEDIA GENERAL FINANCIAL WEEKLY

Published by Media General, Inc.
P.O. Box C-32333
Richmond, VA 23293-0001
Weekly ($108 per year)

This weekly provides detailed statistical data on OTC stocks as well as listed stocks. Comprehensive database.

THE LOW-PRICED STOCK SURVEY

Published by Dow Theory Forecasts, Inc.
7412 Calumet Avenue
Hammond, IN 46324-2692
Published 26 times a year ($25 per year)

Just as its name implies, this publication provides a detailed review, analysis, and recommendations for low-priced (typically OTC) penny stocks for the individual investor.

TURNAROUNDS AND WORKOUTS

Published by Beard Group
P.O. Box 9867
Washington, DC 20016
22 semi-monthly issues ($154 per year)

This publication contains news items and recent court rulings in a wide variety of workout and turnaround situations. Geared for the professional in this area and oriented toward the "smaller" bankruptcies.

GRAHAM-REA REPORT

Published by James B. Rea, Inc.
10966 Chalon Road
Los Angeles, CA 90077
Monthly ($300 per year)

This research report is based on Graham-Rea (value approach) to investing. Detailed information is furnished about high net worth companies and companies selling below book value. Recommendations are made and followed up on a regular basis.

SPECTRUM

Published by CDA Investment Technologies
115-01 Georgia Avenue
Silver Spring, MD 20902
Monthly updates ($975 per year)

This publication lists in alphabetical order holdings and additions or deletions to the major mutual funds, investment advisors, limited partnerships, and insurance companies. The service provides a window to what is of interest to virtually all advisors no matter how small or unknown to the investing public. The service is subscribed to by many public and business libraries.

THE NATIONAL OTC STOCK JOURNAL

Published by The National OTC Stock Journal, Inc.
1780 S. Bellaire Street, Suite 444
Denver, CO 80222
Weekly ($80 per year)

This is one of the more widely followed publications dealing with penny stocks. Its approach is both comprehensive and complete.

PENNY STOCK NEWS

Published by Penny Stock News
8930 J Oakland Center
Columbia, MD 21045
Weekly ($50 per year)

This is a weekly newspaper of the penny-stock world. A typical issue carries a number of articles dealing with the overall market for such issues as well as particular stocks.

THE CHEAP INVESTOR

Published by Bill Matthews
36 King Arthur Court, Suite 10
Northlake, IL 60164
Monthly ($78 per year)

This investment newsletter specializes in stocks selling for under $10—typically the kind of stocks traded OTC. It features a "Blue Cheap Index" consisting of the publisher's favorite stocks. Individual recommendations are made and followed up.

APPENDIX II

The Functioning of the NASD

The National Association of Security Dealers (NASD) was organized under the Maloney Act, an amendment (Section 15A) to the Securities Exchange Act of 1934. Although established by Congress and supervised by the SEC, the NASD operates not as a government agency but as an independent membership association.

PURPOSES OF THE NASD

The NASD's certificate of incorporation, listing its purposes and objectives as shown in Figure II–1, empowers the association to set operating standards to promote just and equitable principles of trade and to require adherence to high standards of commercial honor and integrity.

The NASD's power to regulate lies in its ability to deny membership to any broker/dealer operating in an unethical or improper manner. Because only NASD members have the advantage of price concessions, discounts, and similar

FIGURE II–1. Objectives of the NASD.

To promote the investment banking and securities business.
To standardize principles and practices.
To promote high standards of commercial honor.
To promote the observation of federal and state security laws by members.
To provide a medium through which members may consult with government and other agencies.
To enable members to cooperate with governmental authority in the solution of problems affecting the securities of the industry and investors.
To adopt and enforce rules of fair practice.
To promote just and equitable principles of trade for the protection of investors.
To promote self-discipline among members.
To investigate and adjust grievances between the public and NASD members, as well as between NASD members.

---

allowances, the loss of membership privileges all but prevents a firm from competing in the marketplace. In addition, NASD members are permitted to do business only with other members, although they may deal with foreign banks and dealers.

HOW THE NASD IS ORGANIZED

Board of Governors

The NASD Board of Governors is comprised of 31 members. Some of the members are elected by the board itself, but most are elected by the membership. Each of the NASD's 13 districts elects one or more governors as representatives on the board for three-year terms. The board as a group administers and manages the affairs of the NASD.

District Committees

The members in each of the 13 districts elect a committee, which supervises NASD programs in the district. In addition, it serves as a business conduct committee by doing the following:

- Reviewing the reports of NASD examiners.
- Investigating complaints against members.
- Conducting disciplinary proceedings.
- Imposing penalties for violations of federal and state laws and the NASD's Rules of Fair Practice.

The chairman of each district committee also serves as an advisor to the Board of Governors.

Bylaws

The NASD's bylaws spell out the terms and conditions of everyday operation of the NASD, as well as the classification, qualification, and responsibilities of its members, including the Rules of Fair Practice. The bylaws also deal with such key issues as membership, registration, and qualification standards.

Membership

Membership in the NASD is open to all properly qualified brokers and dealers whose regular course of business is transacted in any branch of the investment banking or securities businesses in the United States. A *broker* is defined as a legal entity (individual, corporation, or partnership) that effects transactions for the accounts of others. A *dealer* is a legal entity that engages in the buying or selling of securities for its own account. All broker/dealers must be registered with the SEC and the state authorities, as required by law, to be eligible for membership in the NASD. By definition, banks are not broker/dealers and are therefore not eligible for NASD membership.

Some broker/dealers may not become members of the NASD, according to the bylaws. Because the main purpose of the NASD is to promote high standards of commercial conduct, broker/dealers convicted of violations of law are barred from membership in the NASD. Specifically, membership is denied to the following:

1. Broker/dealers that have been suspended or expelled from a registered securities association or exchange for acts inconsistent with just and equitable principles of trade.
2. Broker/dealers whose registration with the Securities and Exchange Commission has been revoked or denied.
3. An individual who has been named as a "cause" of a suspension, expulsion, or revocation, or one whose registration as a registered representative has been revoked by the NASD or a national securities exchange.
4. An individual who has been convicted within the preceding ten years of any crime arising out of the securities business and involving embezzlement, fraudulent conversion, misappropriation of funds, or the abuse or misuse of a fiduciary relationship.
5. A broker/dealer whose partner, officer, or employee is not qualified for NASD membership.
6. A broker/dealer with officers, partners, or employees who are required to be registered representatives but who are not.

NASD RULES OF FAIR PRACTICE

The Rules of Fair Practice are a part of the NASD bylaws designed to promote and enforce the highest ethical conduct in the securities business. The most basic of the rules is Section 1, Article III, which states the fundamental philosophy of the NASD: "a member in the conduct of his business, shall observe high standards of commercial honor and just and equitable principles of trade."

The broad-based Rules of Fair Practice include specific rules on many areas of the securities business. Some of the areas addressed by the rules are as follows:

NASD Member Firm Advertising

The Rules of Fair Practice consider it a violation for a member to publish, circulate, or distribute any advertisement, sales literature, or market letter that a member knows to contain untrue, false, or misleading statements. Similarly, no material fact or qualification can be omitted from advertising material if such an omission causes the material to be misleading. In short, all advertising, sales, and market literature must be based on the principles of fair dealing and good faith.

Execution of Retail Trades

So that all customers may benefit from a free and open market, NASD members must use "reasonable diligence"—that is, consider all pertinent factors—to make sure that the customer gets the best possible price under prevailing market conditions. The rules also state that a member's obligation to do the best for customers is not fulfilled by channeling business through another broker/dealer, unless using a third party reduces costs to the customer.

Receipt and Delivery of Securities

No member may accept a customer's purchase order for any security without first making sure that the customer agrees to receive those securities against payment. On the sell side, no member may sell securities for a customer without being reasonably sure that the customer possesses the securities and will deliver them within five business days. To satisfy the requirement of "reasonable assurance," the broker/dealer or registered representative should note on the order ticket the present location of the securities to be sold.

FIGURE II–2. Sections in the Rules of Fair Practice.

Section 1: *Business Conduct of Members.* The broad directive is to "observe high standards of commercial honor and just and equitable principles of trade." Outlined here are the conditions for accepting buy orders in a cash account, sell orders, or short sale orders, as well as directions for handling proxy materials.

Section 2: *Recommendations as to Customers.* This section stresses (1) knowing your customer and (2) obtaining the essential facts about a customer on a new account report form. The purpose is to provide the customer with *fair treatment* and intelligent counsel.

Section 3: *Charges for Services Performed.* Any fees must be reasonable and not unfairly discriminatory. Fees may include charges for collecting dividend or interest payments, tendering securities, registering certificates, subscriptions for new securities offered via rights or warrants, and so on.

Section 4: *Fair Prices and Commissions.* Members are directed to establish *fair and reasonable* markups, markdowns, or commissions. This section contains the 5-percent guidelines policy.

Section 5: *Publication of Transactions and Quotations.* False quotations and prices are forbidden. Nominal subject or nonbinding quotations, if used, must be identified as such. Using nominal quotations to force the contraparty to reveal a position—as a buyer or seller—is not permitted.

Members may not quote securities in newspapers, on the radio, or on television except under certain conditions. Only interdealer quotations (the inside market) may be published, not retail markups, markdowns, or commissions. Nominal quotations or quotations without bid prices may not be published for public information under any circumstances.

Section 6: *Offers at Stated Prices.* A dealer who makes a firm quotation for a security must be prepared to transact business at that price in the security's normal trading unit. Reneging, or backing away, violates principles of fair practice.

Section 7: *Disclosure of Price in Selling Agreements.* Underwriting syndicate and selling group agreements must disclose (1) the public offering price and (2) to whom and under what circumstances any price concessions may be allowed.

FIGURE II–2. Sections in the Rules of Fair Practice (cont'd.).

Section 8: *Securities Taken in Trade.* This section is designed to discourage dealers from swapping at artificial prices. A member offering securities at a fixed price, through either a syndicate or a selling group, may purchase other securities in trade (swap) from customers only (1) at fair market prices prevailing at that time or (2) if the member acts as agent in the transaction, charging a normal commission.

Example: If a member pays an inflated price for another issue in a customer's portfolio, the customer then has enough funds to purchase another security being offered by the members at a high public offering price. Although the member loses some money disposing of the customer's issue at the low prevailing market price, the markup on the public offering is high enough to make an overall profit. But because the customer receives an artificial price for the first security, this practice, often referred to as *overtrading* or *highballing*, violates this section.

Section 9: *Information Obtained as a Fiduciary.* Anyone serving as a transfer agent, disbursement agent, trustee, or in a similar capacity has access to information about the ownership of securities. These agents may not use such information to induce purchases, sales, or exchanges in the issues, unless requested to do so by the issuing corporation.

Section 10: *Influencing or Rewarding Employees of Other Firms.* Members or their employees may not give any gift of more than $25 per person, per year (in cash or merchandise) to someone representing or associated with a customer, if the gratuity is related to business accepted from from the recipient or from the recipient's employer. Bona fide employment contracts for services rendered are not subject to this limitation.

In some cases, registered representatives are paid commissions after they leave the employ of a broker/dealer; even after their deaths, survivors may be paid their commissions. Commissions may be paid, however, *only* if a bona fide contract was drawn up and signed by the rep while employed with the paying firm.

Section 11: *Payment to Influence Market Prices.* Except for legitimate paid advertising practices, members may not give anything of value to someone to influence or to reward comment in

FIGURE II–2. Sections in the Rules of Fair Practice (cont'd.).

a public medium that may affect the market price of a security.

Section 12: *Disclosures on Confirmations.* Upon or before the completion of a customer's transaction, a member must furnish the customer with a confirmation that, among other things, states (1) whether the member acted as principal, as agent for the customer or for another person, or as agent for the customer and another person; (2) on principal transactions, whether the member is a market-maker in the issue; (3) on agency transactions, the contraparty's name and all commissions on the transaction.

Members who execute orders in listed securities in the third market and who act as brokers in such transactions are frequently charged an 1/8-point fee over the going price on the exchange by the market-maker. If the member intends to pay the fee out of the commission charged on the transaction, the member must notify the customer in a legend on the confirmation.

Section 13: *Disclosure of Control.* Broker/dealers who control, or who are controlled by, the issuer of a security must disclose that fact in writing to the customer before completing any transaction in the issue.

Section 14: *Disclosure of Participation in Primary or Secondary Distributions.* If a broker/dealer participates in or has a financial interest in the primary or secondary distribution of any security offering, the representative must tell the customer in writing before completing the transaction.

Section 15: *Discretionary Accounts.* Registered representatives may not exercise discretionary power in any account unless (1) they have written authorization from the customer and (2) written acceptance is evidenced by the initials of a registered principal of the member firm. Even then, each discretionary order must be initialed promptly by a registered principal, and the account must be reviewed at frequent intervals to ensure against churning or transactions beyond the customer's financial capability.

The restrictions on "discretion" do not apply to the use of judgment regarding the price or time of execution, when the customer, either orally or in writing, requests such discretion.

FIGURE II–2. Sections in the Rules of Fair Practice (cont'd.).

Section 16: *Offerings at the Market.* Sometimes a member participates or has a financial interest in the primary or secondary distribution of a security that is not trading on a national securities exchange. In this case, the firm may represent the security as a *market offering* or as an offering *at the market,* if the member is the only market-maker for the issue. "Market" terms imply a competitive situation, and only one market-maker does not constitute such a situation.

Section 17: *Solicitation of Purchases on an Exchange to Facilitate Distribution of Securities.* When a broker/dealer participates in the distribution of a security or has a financial interest in a security, it may not offer any *special* compensation or inducement to get the security bought and sold on a national exchange.

Section 18: *Use of Fraudulent Devices.* Manipulative, deceptive, or other fraudulent devices are specifically prohibited. A *boiler room* is a high-pressure sales set up with many canvassers using telephone books and purchased mailing lists to solicit customers for securities of little value, such as those issued by asset-less shell corporations. A *bucket shop* is a brokerage firm that accepts but does not immediately execute customers' orders, hoping that market values will fluctuate against the customers' interest. The firm bills the customers at the unfavorable prices while executing at profit prices, pocketing the difference for itself.

Section 19: *Customers, Securities, and Funds.* NASD members and employees are forbidden to make improper use of a customer's securities or funds. Specifically prohibited are (1) pledging or lending a customer's securities improperly, (2) improperly holding fully paid securities in cash accounts or excess collateral securities in margin accounts, (3) guaranteeing customers against loss in any securities transactions, (4) sharing in the profits or losses in any customer account, except under certain circumstances.

Section 20: *Installment or Partial Payment Sales.* Customers may not pay for their purchases in installments, or even over a period of time, unless (1) Reg T requirements are satisfied and (2) the member firm possesses or controls the securities while the obligation is outstanding.

FIGURE II–2. Sections in the Rules of Fair Practice (cont'd.).

Section 21: *Books and Records.* Each member has to keep and preserve any records applying to account information, in addition to a complaint file.

Section 22: *Disclosure of Financial Condition.* Broker/dealers must send their customers certain annual financial statements dealing with, among other points, the firm's subordinated losses, its required and actual net capital, and material deficiencies (if any). Every six months, the firm must send its customers an uncertified balance sheet and a statement of the firm's net and required net capital.

This section also defines customer as any person for whom, or with whom, the first (1) has executed a transaction or (2) holds or owes money or securities.

Section 23: *Net Prices to Persons Not in Investment Banking, or Securities Business.* When dealing with someone who is not in investment banking or the securities business, members may not offer any discount, concession, or other allowance.

Section 24: *Selling Concessions.* Selling concessions, discounts, or other price allowances are permitted only for services rendered in the distribution of securities. So they may be granted only to broker/dealers engaged in investment banking or the securities business.

Section 25: *Dealing with Nonmembers.* Members must deal with nonmember broker/dealers at the same prices, commissions, fees, terms, and conditions accorded to the general public. This rule does not apply to (1) foreign broker/dealers, under certain conditions, (2) transactions on a national securities exchange with exchange members, or (3) transactions in certain exempted securities.

This last exception does not extend to municipal securities. Banks and the municipal securities departments of banks, however, are not defined as "broker/dealers." So they can and often do get favorable treatment from NASD members in municipal securities activities.

Section 26: *Investment Companies.* This section stipulates what members may or may not do in the offering and distribution of open-end managementries (mutual funds).

FIGURE II–2. Sections in the Rules of Fair Practice (cont'd.).

This section also requires that mutual fund sales charges should be "fair and reasonable." Although the markup is exempted from the 5-percent guidelines, a sales charge higher than 8.5% of the offering price is considered excessive and the maximum charge is usually close to 6% of the offering price.

Section 27: *Supervision.* Members must maintain written procedures to ensure their employees' compliance with securities laws, regulations, and NASD policies. At least one office in the firm, called Office of Supervisory Jurisdiction (OSJ) and managed by a registered principal, must be responsible for reviewing the firm's compliance activities.

Section 28: *Transactions for Personnel of Another Member.* To accept an order for an employee or principal of another NASD firm, the executing firm must have written approval to open and maintain an account from the employer or fellow principal.

Section 29: *Variable Contracts of an Insurance Company.* A *variable contract* is an investment program whose value varies according to the performance of a portfolio maintained by an insurance company. This type of program is sold by broker/dealer affiliates of insurance companies or by broker/dealers licensed to sell insurance. The guidelines for marketing and sales charges for these programs are similar to those for mutual funds.

Section 30: *Margin Accounts.* This section establishes minimum initial and maintenance margin requirements, which may be more stringent than the Fed's Reg T requirements. NASD members that are also members of a principal U.S. stock exchange are exempted from the NASD rule.

Section 31: *Failed-to-Deliver Contracts.* An *aged fail-to-deliver contract* is a transaction between brokerage firms that has not settled by delivery and payment for a 60-day period after the settlement date. (For foreign securities, the period is 90 days. Exempted securities are not affected by this section.) When a member has an aged failed-to-deliver contract, its registered representatives may not buy as agent for customer accounts or sell the security as principal for proprietary accounts.

FIGURE II–2. Sections in the Rules of Fair Practice (cont'd.).

Section 32: *Blanket Fidelity Bond.* If a member has employees and is required to join SIPC, it is subject to SEC net capital rules and must purchase and maintain fidelity bond insurance.

Section 33: *Securities Options.* The NASD Board of Governors is authorized to adopt, alter, amend, supplement, or modify rules relating to transactions in OTC options, as well as any listed options displayed on the NASDAQ system.

Section 34: *Direct Participation (Tax-Sheltered) Programs.* Direct participation programs refer to such investments as oil and gas drilling ventures, real estate syndicates (except REITs), citrus grove development, or cattle breeding programs. This section prescribes standards for such programs.

Section 35: *Communication with the Public—Advertising Practices.* Sales literature, market letters, and recruiting materials (except in-house intrafirm materials, tombstones, personal recommendations to clients) may not contain false or misleading statements of any material facts. nor may such communications purposely omit important information. The section prescribes guidelines for acceptable content and approved procedures in preparing these communications.

Section 36: *Transactions with Related Persons.* Distributors of fixed-price offerings, such as corporate security underwritings, may not sell those issues to "related persons" unless all public demand has been satisfied. A "related person" is an entity that owns, or is owned by, an NASD member.

Section 37: *Best-Efforts Underwritings (Proposed).* The effect of this section is to eliminate price manipulation in secondary market activity while the security offering is still in progress. It further ensures the availability of enough certificates to reduce potential for premium prices and fail-to-deliver contracts between members when trading is permitted.

Section 38: *Underwriting Inquiry Standards (Proposed).* Because investment banking members must "perform due diligence" before underwriting a securities issue, this section contains guidelines to ensure adequate investigation. The investigation of tax-sheltered programs calls for additional steps.

Forwarding of Reports and Proxy Material

When securities are held for a customer by a brokerage firm, they are usually held in *street name* (that is, in the name of the broker/dealer). In these cases, the issuer of the security sends all literature, including reports and proxies, to the brokerage firm, not to the customers. If NASD member firms do not promptly forward such material to customers, their conduct can be regarded as inconsistent with high standards of commercial honor.

Recommendations to Customers

According to the Rules of Fair Practice, all recommendations to a customer to purchase, sell, or exchange securities must be based on reasonable grounds and be suitable for the customer's account: The controlling factor is the best interest of the customer. To determine suitability, the member is expected to learn about the specific financial condition and needs of each customer. Specific violations of this section of the rules are listed in Figure II–3.

NASD UNIFORM PRACTICE CODE

The Uniform Practice Code (UPC) is a part of the NASD bylaws whose purpose is the uniformity of the customs, practices, and trading techniques used among all NASD members. The code includes rules for trade terms, the delivery of securities, payment, rights, stamp taxes, computation of interest, and due bills.

The administration of the UPC is the responsibility of the National Uniform Practice Committee and the District Uniform Practice Committees. Any changes in the rules by district committees must be approved by the board. Any contract between NASD members (except transactions in exempt securities or on national exchanges) is subject to the Uniform Practice Code.

FIGURE II–3. Violations of the Suitability Rule.

1. Members should not recommend low-priced, speculative securities if they do not know the customer's other holdings, financial situation, and other relevant information. For example, a low-priced security may be suitable for a wealthy investor with large holdings who understands the risk. The same investment would not be suitable for a person of modest means on a fixed income with no other investments.
2. Creating excessive activity in a customer's account to generate commission is a violation known as *churning* or *overtrading*.
3. Trading in mutual fund shares is a violation of the Rules of Fair Practice. Mutual fund shares are considered long-term investments, and many funds charge a sales commission (or "load") on purchase. They are therefore clearly not trading vehicles, and trading these shares does not benefit the customer.
4. Members may not establish "fictitious" accounts to execute trades that would otherwise be prohibited, such as purchases of hot issues.
5. Members may not execute transactions that are not authorized by the customer.
6. Members may not use or borrow customers' securities without authorization from the customer.
7. Registered reps may not conceal transactions from the member firm that employs them.
8. No member can recommend the purchase of securities in amounts greater than the customer's financial ability to pay for them.

If a situation arises that is not specifically covered by the written code, it is referred to the appropriate District Uniform Practice Committee for action. Controversies about an inter-district trade are referred to the National Uniform Practice Committee.

Some of the important sections of the UPC are as follows:

Delivery of Securities

For each security transaction, there are two key dates: the trade date and the delivery date.

Trade Date. The transaction takes place on the trade date. The NASD code requires that all ordinary transactions be confirmed in writing on or before the first full business day following the trade date.

Delivery Date. The delivery date is the date on which securities should be delivered to the customer. There are several types of delivery:

- *Cash:* Settlement occurs on the same day as the trade itself. Cash settlement is used when the client has to settle a transaction before a certain date, such as year end for tax purposes.
- *Next day:* The contract is settled the first business day after the trade date.
- *Regular way:* The seller agrees to deliver the securities to the office of the buyer on the fifth full business day following the transaction date.
- *Seller's option:* For securities other than U.S. government securities, this type of delivery allows the seller to have the securities at the buyer's office on the business day that the seller's option expires.

  Example: If securities are sold "seller's 30," the seller can deliver up to 30 days from the trade date, as long as one day's notice is given and five business days have elapsed from the trade date.

- This type of delivery is often requested by sellers who have difficulty getting possession of their securities.
- *Buyer's option:* This type of delivery gives the buyer the option to receive securities on a specific date.

Five-day (regular way) delivery applies to most trades in over-the-counter securities and securities listed on an exchange. All corporate, municipal, and most federal agency securities trade the regular way. United States government securities may be delivered, regular way, next day, and the seller's option of not less than two nor more than 60 days.

Don't Know (DK) Procedures

After a trade, each broker/dealer sends the other a notice to confirm the details. If both parties recognize and acknowledge the trade, it is *confirmed*, or *compared*. Sometimes, however, the contrabroker (the broker/dealer with whom the trade was made) sends back a signed *DK*, a *don't know* notice, telling the confirming broker that the contrabroker does not "know"—or recognize—the trade. If the contrabroker does not respond to the confirming broker by the close of four business days from the trade date, the following procedures can be used:

1. Not later than the fifteenth calendar day after the trade date, the confirming member sends a DK notice to the contrabroker.
2. The contrabroker then has four business days after the notice is received either to confirm or to DK the transaction.
3. Failure to receive a response from the contrabroker by the close of four business days constitutes a DK, and the confirming member has no further liability.
4. All DK notices sent by either party must be signed by authorized persons.

A DK is sometimes referred to as a *questioned trade* (QT).

Dividends

When a corporation declares a dividend, there are four significant dates as follows:

1. The *declaration date* is the date on which the corporation declares a dividend to common or preferred shareholders.

2. The *record date* is the date on which the corporation's recorded shareholders are listed for purposes of paying the declared dividend.
3. The *ex-dividend date* is the date on or after which the buyer of stock is *not* entitled to receive a declared dividend.
4. The *payment date* is the day on which the dividend is actually paid to shareholders.

Securities normally go *ex-dividend* (that is, without dividend) on the fourth business day preceding the record date. *Anyone purchasing the securities on or after the ex-dividend date is not entitled to receive the dividend.*

> ***Example:*** Gyrus Corporation declares a dividend to be paid to holders of record on February 10, a Monday; this is the record date. Anyone buying the stock has to buy it at least five days before the record date in order to take delivery and be recorded as the owner. To be the holder of record, you have to purchase Gyrus on or by February 3 (seven calendar days or five business days before delivery). Gyrus starts trading ex-dividend on February 4.

Due Bills

Occasionally, a security is sold before the ex-dividend date but is delivered too late for the buying broker to record ownership and get the dividend. In this case, the selling broker receives the dividend but is actually not entitled to keep it. At the time of the sale, the buyer can demand a promise from the seller to pay the dividend. This claim on dividends is called a *due bill.*

Good Delivery

To assure clear ownership, the NASD Uniform Practice Code requires that all transactions must be for *good delivery*—that is, the security must be in proper form so that the record of ownership may be readily transferred. The qualifications for good delivery are as follows:

1. Stock certificates must be accompanied by an assignment. For example, if a stock certificate is registered in the name of John A. Smith, the owner must endorse the certificate exactly that way.

   The assignment (endorsement) can be made in the appropriate space on the back of the certificate. Or if a registered stockholder does not have the certificate available, a stock power can be used.

   If a certificate is issued in the name of joint tenants or tenants in common, the delivery is good only if the certificate is signed by all co-tenants. Sometimes a *power of substitution* is used, in which the owner assigns power of attorney to the broker to facilitate transfer.
2. The certificate must be in good condition.
3. When a contract is for more than 100 shares, the delivered certificates must be in denominations from which units of 100 shares can be made. For example, a trade for 300 shares can be satisfied by three certificates for 100 shares or six certificates for 50 shares. But four certificates for 75 shares are not good delivery because the pieces cannot be bunched into lots of 100 shares. For odd lots, the exact number of shares must be delivered.
4. A certificate in the name of a deceased person is not good delivery, even if it is properly assigned. Such certificates must be transferred to the executor of the estate or to street name.
5. A bond or preferred stock that is called for redemption is not good delivery unless the entire issue has been called.
6. Temporary certificates are not good delivery if permanent certificates are available.
7. Delivery of bonds should be in denominations of $1000 or in multiples adding up to $1000.

THE NASD CODE OF PROCEDURE

The Code of Procedure is a part of the NASD bylaws providing the rules for administering disciplinary action to members for infractions of the Rules of Fair Practice.

Complaints about violations of the NASD's rules can be filed by any member of the public, by an NASD member, by the district committee itself, or by the Board of Governors. All complaints must be made in writing and must cite the rule or interpretation allegedly violated. The respondent is allowed ten days to answer or refute the accusation. Either party in a complaint has the right to request a hearing at which legal counsel may be present. All trade practice complaints are heard and passed upon first by the District Business Conduct Committee (DBCC), in whose district the respondent's main office is located or where the violation was purported to have taken place. The committee decides the case and determines the appropriate action. The DBCC has the power to censure, fine, suspend, and even expel members.

For minor offenses, the DBCC may offer the accused member a summary complaint proceeding. If the accused member accepts, the member agrees to admit guilt, waive a formal hearing, accept a penalty of censure and/or a fine of up to $2500, and waive all right of appeal before the Board of Governors.

More serious violations are adjudicated by the district committee through a regular procedure involving formal hearings and a trial. The committee's judgments are subject to review by the Board of Governors upon appeal by any participant or on the board's own initiative. The Board of Governors can either uphold, decrease, increase, or modify penalties.

Members not satisfied with the decision of the Board of Governors have the option of appeal outside the NASD, first to the SEC and finally to the public court system.

APPENDIX III

Financial Statement Analysis

Intelligent investment decisions are made after careful consideration of available information: facts about world events, domestic news, industry reports, and corporate announcements. Most investors also rely on financial information released by the company to aid them in their judgments to buy or sell.

Information that comes from the corporation itself is also subject to an investor's interpretation, despite the well-known axiom that "figures don't lie." A corporation with $1 million in total assets and at least 500 stockholders is obliged to file financial information with the Securities and Exchange Commission (SEC) under the Securities Exchange Act of 1934. (Exempt from this rule are banks and insurance companies regulated by state or federal authority, whose rules parallel the SEC's anyway. Also excluded from reporting requirements are corporations engaged in religious, education, fraternal, or other eleemosynary enterprises.) These corporations must report significant events and changes as they occur periodically and must file an audited financial statement with the commission annually. At about the same time, similar information is distributed to the company's shareholders. However, the information is raw, without explanation or analysis. Shareholders and prospective purchasers are expected to know and understand the techniques the company uses to keep the investment community informed.

This is often a difficult task because accounting is not a precise science. It is a sophisticated art, using various methods to present the same basic information and arrive at different conclusions. Despite the fact that most companies follow the standards of the FASB (Financial Accounting Standards Board), there is still enough leeway for accounting practices to vary from company to company, even within the same industry. Frequently, the difference in approach depends on management's judgment; sometimes it depends on the preferences of the auditor who prepares the statements. In any case, anyone who analyzes such information should realize that these documents are only part fact and part opinion.

Nevertheless, valuable insight into the health and wealth of a corporation is often readily apparent from careful examination of that institution's financial reports. A shareholder or registered representative need have only a fundamental knowledge of accounting terms, procedures, and analysis in order to interpret such data competently. This appendix presents and identifies basic information in understandable lay language.

THE BALANCE SHEET

Periodically, a corporation needs to demonstrate to its shareholders what the company is worth. The company simply lists everything it owns (assets) and everything it owes (liabilities). *Assets* are items of value—things that a company *owns* or has *owed to it;* assets are a corporation's possessions, or its pluses. *Liabilities* are the company's obligations—its debts, what the company *owes*. The difference between assets and liabilities represents the company's net worth or the stockholders' net ownership, called *stockholders' equity*. This tabulation of assets, liabilities, and net worth is known as a *balance sheet*. The basic balance sheet equation is

Assets = Liabilities + Stockholders' equity

Both sides balance, of course, because a corporation's stockholders have a stake in their corporation equal to the amount by which the corporation's assets exceed its liabilities. Expressed another way, what a company owns (assets) minus what it owes (liabilities) is equal to its net worth. The net worth (stockholders' equity) represents the value of the shareholders' investment in the corporation: It is the amount of money invested in the business by stockholders, plus the profits that have *not* been paid out as dividends.

Since a firm's financial state is continually changing, the balance sheet must be dated. The balance sheet's date shows on what day the tabulations were made. The assets, liabilities, and stockholders' equity are listed at their values *at the close of business* on the date shown at the top of the statement. A *simplified* balance sheet appears in Table III–1.

The value of the items owned—of the assets—can be figured many different ways. In actuality, the amount of money received from buyers, should all the assets be sold (liquidated), may differ dramatically from the values shown on the balance sheet. The shareholders' (stockholders') equity therefore represents the amount of money that *would* go to the preferred and common stockholders if all the company's assets were sold at the values at which they are carried on the balance sheet and if all liabilities were paid off as well. Thus, in another form, the balance sheet equation is

Shareholders' equity = Total assets – Total liabilities

Let us build a sample balance sheet for a typical manufacturing corporation, a block at a time, explaining each item separately.

TABLE III–1.

BALANCE SHEET
ROXBURY MANUFACTURING COMPANY
December 31, 19X8

Assets	
Cash	$ 75,000
Marketable securities	150,000
Accounts receivable	375,000
Inventory	400,000
Total current assets	$1,000,000
Property, plant, and equipment	$ 605,000
Prepayments	20,000
Intangibles	10,000
Total assets	$1,635,000

=

Liabilities	
Accounts payable	$200,000
Accrued expenses	150,000
Accrued taxes	50,000
Total current liabilities	$400,000
Bonds—8%, due 19Z5	500,000
Total liabilities	$900,000

+

Stockholders' Equity	
Preferred stock—6% ($100 par)	$ 75,000
Common stock ($10 par)	300,000
Capital surplus	100,000
Retained earnings	260,000
Total stockholders' equity	$ 735,000
Total liabilities and stockholders' equity	$1,635,000

Assets

A corporation's assets are traditionally listed, by type, in the following order:

1. Current assets
2. Fixed assets
3. Sundry assets
4. Intangibles

Current Assets. These are items that a company owns or has owed to it and that, in the normal course of business, will be converted into cash within a year or less. This category includes:

- *Cash.* In addition to bank deposits, these are the bills and coins in the corporate "till." Such deposits are usually of the demand type, such as *checking* account balances.
- *Marketable securities.* Cash that the company does not need immediately it puts to work by investing it, usually in short-term instruments such as Treasury bills. The value of such investments is shown on the balance sheet at the *lower* of their cost or their market value; in the vast majority of cases the market value of the securities is higher than their cost, so cost usually appears on the balance sheet. An indication elsewhere, possibly in a footnote, cites the current market value of the securities.
- *Accounts receivable.* Most manufacturing companies sell to wholesalers or distributors. Goods are usually shipped with payment expected within 15 to 90 days. The total amount of billings outstanding represents the amount of money due the company for goods already shipped. Since the *entire* amount of the billings will probably not be collected for various reasons (for example, bankruptcy of the buyer), an estimate of bad debts is made. This *allowance for bad debt* is deducted from the total accounts receivable, and the leftover figure is shown on the balance

sheet. This net figure represents an estimate of the amount that will be collected eventually.

- *Inventory.* This category includes raw materials, work in progress, and finished goods. Like marketable securities, inventories are carried on the balance sheet at the lower of cost or market value. Except in very unusual situations, the market value of the inventory is expected to be higher than its cost: A manufacturing corporation makes its profit selling its finished goods for more than it costs to produce them. Cost accounting for inventory is based on two popular methods: FIFO (first-in/first-out) and LIFO (last-in/first-out). The method that a company chooses can have a dramatic effect on its earnings and on the value of the inventory remaining after a sale.

  Example: Roxbury Manufacturing has three manufactured items in inventory, each one produced in successive months at successively higher costs. During inflationary periods, such a situation is the norm. The first item manufactured (the one longest in inventory) cost $100, the second item cost $110, and the last item cost $120. The company is now selling its products for $300 each. Under FIFO the gross profit is $200, since the item sold is considered to be the first item produced at a cost of $100. The value of the inventory remaining after the sale totals $230. Under the LIFO method, the profit on $300 is based on the last item produced (at a cost of $120), and the gross profit is therefore only $180. The remaining inventory valuation is $210.

During *inflationary* periods, therefore, the FIFO method yields higher profits (and higher taxes!) than LIFO. FIFO also results in higher inventory evaluation. During *deflationary* periods, the results are just the opposite. Figure III–1 gives you a visual aid in remembering the effects of LIFO over FIFO during inflationary periods.

Total Current Assets. The sum of these four types of current assets is the corporation's *total current assets.* Now more

FIGURE III–1. Inventory Cost Accounting.

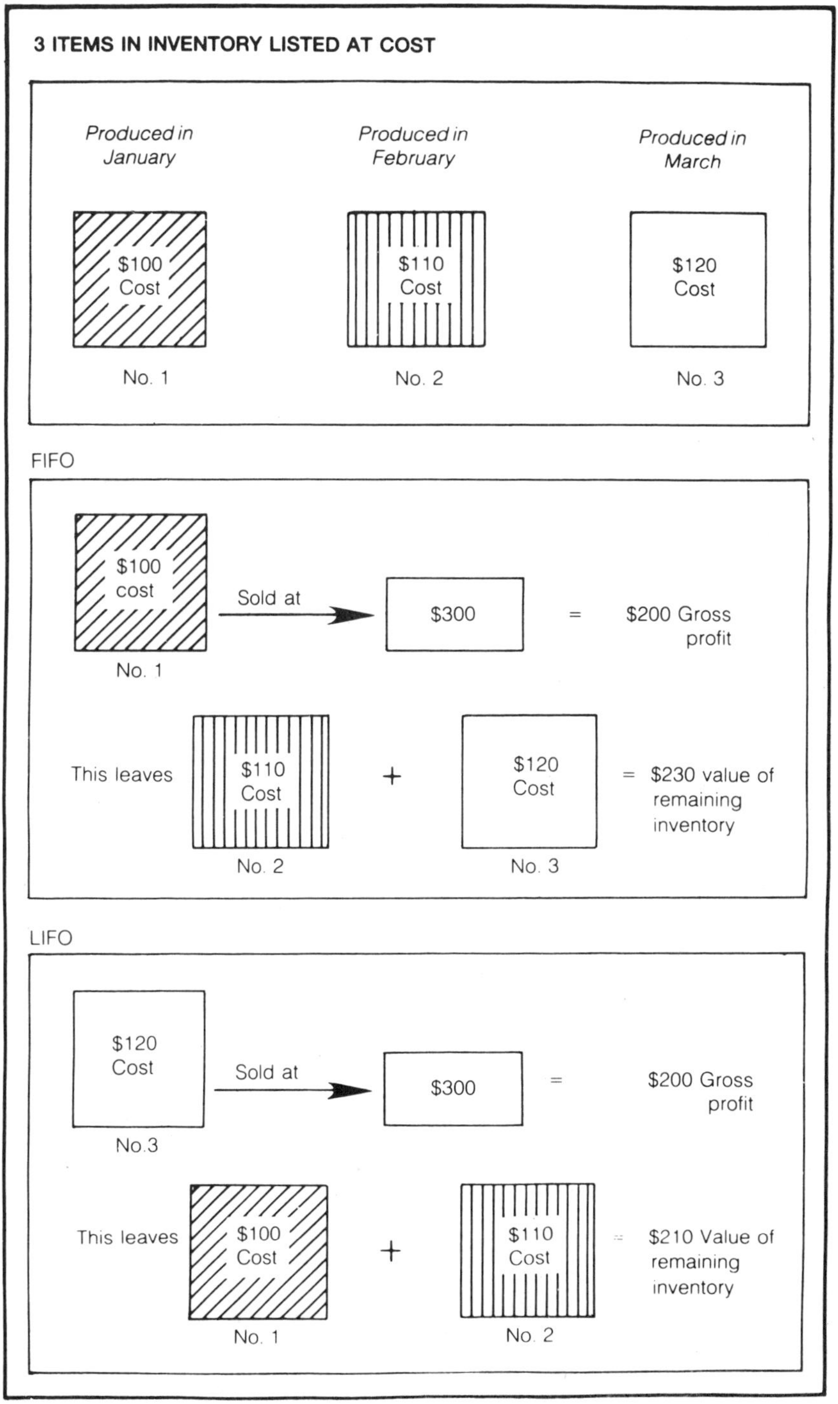

detail can be added to the current asset portion of the sample balance sheet in Table III–1. Compare the section below with the first section in that figure. Note that some corporate balance sheets might show such additional items as notes receivable and/or prepaid expenses. Prepaid expenses are explained in this appendix.

Current Assets	
Cash	$ 75,000
Marketable securities at cost	
(Market value—$156,000)	150,000
Accounts receivable	
($390,000 less $15,000 allowance for bad debt)	375,000
Inventory (first-in/first-out)	400,000
Total current assets	$ 1,000,000

Current assets are in constant motion. When a company sells its products, an appropriate amount is deducted from inventory and goes into accounts receivable. When buyers pay their bills, accounts receivable become cash and the cash may then be used to pay debts. Or, a company may add to inventory and thus repeat the cycle.

Also, when an item is sold for more than its inventoried value, the difference (that is, the *gross profit*) automatically increases the total current assets by the amount of the profit. (How this profit is reflected is demonstrated on the *other* side of the balance sheet later.) Since both sides must balance, this profit is reflected by a corresponding increase in shareholders' equity. The company has made a profit, and the shareholders are therefore better off.

Quick Assets. The total current assets that may be *quickly* converted into cash, should the company deem it necessary, are called *quick assets.* The only item under current assets that is *not* considered very liquid is inventory. Therefore, to figure *quick assets,* merely subtract inventory from total current assets.

Example:

Cash	$ 75,000
Marketable securities	150,000
Accounts receivable	375,000
Inventory	400,000
Total current assets	$1,000,000

Subtracting inventory ($400,000) from the total ($1,000,000) leaves a figure of $600,000 for quick assets. Of course, the same amount may be derived by adding together cash, marketable securities, and accounts receivable—if these figures are all you have to work with. The formulas are as follows:

Quick assets = Total current assets – Inventory
= $1,000,000 – $400,000
= $600,000

or

Quick assets = Cash + Marketable securities
+ Accounts receivable
= $75,000 + $150,000 + $375,000
= $600,000

Fixed Assets. The items of value used in current operations that can be expected to generate revenue are referred to as *fixed assets*. Included in this category are such items as improved land, buildings, furniture and fixtures, machinery, tools, and transportation equipment—sometimes referred to collectively as *property, plant,* and *equipment*. These assets are normally not considered as items to be sold but rather as "tools of the trade" with which the manufactured product is produced, displayed, and transported. Most fixed assets are listed on the balance sheet as *cost minus accumulated depreciation*. For our typical manufacturing corporation the fixed assets are $605,000, as shown on the balance sheet under property, plant, and equipment. (*See* Table III–1.)

Depreciation. As fixed assets grow older, they decrease in value due to ordinary wear and tear, action of the elements, or obsolescence. Since the balance sheet attempts to list everything owned by the corporation at current value, the value at which fixed assets are shown declines as the assets get older. When a fixed asset is acquired by the corporation, it is *not* charged as a business expense in the year it is purchased. Since a fixed asset is expected to last quite a few years, the company charges it as an expense, *a little at a time,* spread over the years it is supposed to be usable to the company. By way of analogy, assume you as an individual wanted to spread out a personal expense of $5,000 for a car. Instead of considering your car expense for one year to be $5,000 and nothing for each additional year you own the car, you might consider your expense to be $1,000 a year for five consecutive years, thus spreading out the expense. Spreading out the expense is what is done by a corporation! The amount by which the fixed assets are lowered each year is the portion of the cost of fixed assets charged as an expense for a given year; that portion is called *annual depreciation* and is listed as such.

Fixed assets may be depreciated by three principal methods:

1. Straight-line
2. Sum-of-years' digits
3. Double declining balance

When a fixed asset is purchased, the company determines how long the asset is expected to be used (*useful life*). It also determines the value that it expects to receive when the asset is scrapped (*salvage value*). The cost of the asset is considered to be the initial price *minus* the salvage value, because the salvage value will be received some time after the item is purchased. In most cases, this net cost figure is the amount depreciated over the item's useful life, not the full price paid. The simple equation is

$$\text{Net cost} = \text{Actual cost} - \text{Salvage value}$$

Depreciation for tax purposes is not computed in the same way as depreciation for financial accounting purposes.

> ***Example:*** In each of the following examples for determining the amount of depreciation, the fixed asset is purchased for \$40,000; it is expected to have a useful life of five years and a salvage value of \$10,000.

$$\begin{aligned}\text{Net cost} &= \text{Actual cost} - \text{Salvage value}\\ &= \$40{,}000 - \$10{,}000\\ &= \$30{,}000\end{aligned}$$

Straight-line depreciation is the simplest and most commonly used method. To determine the amount of each year's depreciation, divide the *net* cost of the item (actual cost – salvage value) by the number of years of useful life.

$$\begin{aligned}\text{Annual depreciation} &= \frac{\text{Net cost}}{\text{Years of useful life}}\\ &= \frac{\$30{,}000}{5} = \$6{,}000\end{aligned}$$

Fixed assets are carried at *cost less accumulated depreciation*. At the end of the item's first year of use, the fixed asset section of the balance sheet shows:

Fixed Assets		
Cost	\$40,000	
Accumulated depreciation	– 6,000	
		\$34,000

The annual writeoff (depreciation) is the same in years 2 through 5. At the end of the second year, the *accumulated depreciation* is \$12,000 (\$6,000 from year 1 plus \$6,000 from year 2), and the balance sheet shows:

Fixed Assets		
Cost	$40,000	
Accumulated depreciation	– 12,000	
		$28,000

By year 5, accumulated depreciation totals up to $30,000, and the asset has been "written down" to a carrying value of $10,000, its salvage value. The total picture in chart form is shown in Table III–2.

TABLE III–2. Straight-Line Depreciation.

Year		*Annual Depreciation*	*Accumulated Depreciation*	*Asset's Balance Sheet Value*
1	$ 30,000 ÷ 5 =	$ 6,000	$ 6,000	$34,000
2	30,000 ÷ 5 =	6,000	12,000	28,000
3	30,000 ÷ 5 =	6,000	18,000	22,000
4	30,000 ÷ 5 =	6,000	24,000	16,000
5	30,000 ÷ 5 =	6,000	30,000	10,000

Note that each year's depreciation is 20% of the net cost of the fixed asset since you are working with a useful life of 5 years (100% ÷ 5 = 20%).

Tax depreciation for federal income tax purposes is determined using the accelerated cost recovery system (ACRS). Taxpayers who are entitled to depreciate fixed assets and other capital equipment now have a choice of straight line and ACRS. In addition, the IRS also distinguishes between real property—what you and I would call real estate—and personal property, which you and I would call equipment such as automobiles, computers, and other similar items.

Sundry Assets. This is a *miscellaneous* category, generally including unimproved land, prepaid expenses, deferred charges, and other items that are usually considered investments for the future. *Prepaid expenses* include payments for materials or services in *advance* of their receipt or use, such as early rent payments and insurance premiums. *Deferred charges* are used to "charge off" major expenses, such as those incurred in the introduction of a new product or the formation of a new subsidiary company.

> *Example:* A company spends $1,000,000 to purchase a ten-year lease in a given year. It includes $900,000 in the sundry assets section so that the *total assets* section shows a decline of only $100,000 that year; that is, the company considers $900,000 of the total amount spent as an asset in terms of having a lease. The balance sheet shows cash minus $1,000,000 and sundry assets plus $900,000. The company then reduces the $900,000 in each subsequent year for the next nine years so that it spreads out the $1,000,000 cost for the lease over a ten-year period.

Intangible Assets. Included in this category are items of value that have no physical existence, such as patents, franchises, and goodwill. Such items are very difficult to quantify. Traditionally, intangibles are the last item shown on the asset side of the balance sheet.

Liabilities

Let us now turn our attention to the *right* (debit) side of the balance sheet. Here are listed the corporation's debts and, further down, the stockholders' equity.

Current Liabilities. Now shift to the *other* side of the balance sheet to look at the debts of the corporation that are scheduled for payment within one year. This quick comparison determines in a shorthand way, as accountants do, whether enough money is available to stay in business. Since current assets, at least in theory, represent the source from which current liabilities are paid, you want to know how the debts compare with the assets.

Current liabilities might include: *accounts payable*, the amount the company owes to its business creditors; *accrued expenses*, amounts owed to its salespeople in salaries and wages, interest on debt, and all other unpaid items; *accrued taxes*, federal, state, and local taxes owed, social security (FICA) deductions, and local government levies withheld from employees; *notes payable*, monies owed to banks, to other lenders, or on outstanding bonds that are due to be paid within the year. The current liabilities section of the balance sheet of our typical manufacturing corporation reads:

Accounts payable	$200,000
Accrued expenses	150,000
Accrued taxes	+ 50,000
Total current liabilities	$400,000

Relating Current Assets to Current Liabilities

Working Capital. The relationship between current assets and current liabilities is quite important. After all, a corporation must be able to keep current on its obligations. At a minimum, there should be an excess of current assets over current liabilities. This excess, called *working capital*, represents the amount of money that would be left from the current assets if all current liabilities were paid off. This important figure is derived by subtracting current liabilities from current assets, thus:

$$\text{Working capital} = \text{Current assets} - \text{Current liabilities}$$

A company's ability to meet its obligations is measured, at least in part, by the amount of its working capital. Working capital is also known as *net working capital* or *net current assets*.

Example:

Assets		*Liabilities*	
Cash	$ 75,000	Accounts payable	$200,000
Marketable securities	150,000	Accrued expenses	150,000
Accounts receivable	375,000	Accrued taxes	50,000
Inventory	+ 400,000		+
Total current assets	$1,000,000	Total current liabilities	$400,000

For our typical corporation:

Working capital = Current assets – Current liabilities
= $1,000,000 – $400,000
= $600,000

Current Ratio. Working with a *dollar* figure for working capital is difficult, especially when comparing one company with another. Dollars alone do not tell the whole story. A company may have only a modest amount of working capital. Or its current liabilities may be very large, requiring many more dollars of working capital for safety's sake. Of primary importance, therefore, is the *proportion* by which current assets exceed current liabilities. This ratio, called the *current ratio,* is arrived at by dividing current assets by current liabilities. Thus:

$$\text{Current ratio} = \frac{\text{Current assets}}{\text{Current liabilities}}$$

Using the figures from the previous section on working capital:

$$\text{Current ratio} = \frac{\$1,000,000}{\$400,000} = 2.5$$

The current ratio, 2.5, means that our typical corporation can cover its current liabilities two and a half times over. In other words, for every dollar of current liabilities, it has $2^{1}/_{2}$ dollars of current assets.

This current ratio is expressed in a variety of ways:

2.5 or $2^{1}/_{2}$ or 2.5 x or $2^{1}/_{2}$ times or
2.5 to 1 or $2^{1}/_{2}$ to 1 or $2^{1}/_{2}$ /1

A good current ratio for a typical manufacturing company is 2 to 1 or higher. For a company with easily collectible receivables, like a public utility, a current ratio as low as 1 to 1 may be acceptable.

Quick Asset Ratio. An even more stringent test of a company's ability to meet its current obligations is the *quick asset ratio,* also called the *liquidity ratio* or *acid test ratio.* This ratio indicates the relationship between *quick assets* and current liabilities:

$$\text{Quick asset ratio} = \frac{\text{Quick assets}}{\text{Current liabilities}}$$

Example: Using the ongoing figures for our corporation:

$$\begin{aligned}\text{Quick assets} &= \text{Total current assets} - \text{Inventory}\\ &= \$1{,}000{,}000 - \$400{,}000\\ &= \$600{,}000\end{aligned}$$

$$\begin{aligned}\text{Quick asset ratio} &= \frac{\text{Quick assets}}{\text{Total current liabilities}}\\ &= \frac{\$600{,}000}{\$400{,}000} = 1.5\end{aligned}$$

The quick asset ratio of 1.5 indicates that our corporation has one and one half times the total of its short-term liabilities in quick assets alone. A safe quick asset ratio for the average manufacturing concern is 1 to 1. In other words, the corporation should have enough *quick* assets to pay off all the current liabilities.

Fixed Liabilities. The fixed liabilities appear below current liabilities on the balance sheet. The major item, ordinarily, is the corporation's funded debt, usually outstanding bonds maturing more than one year in the future. This category may also include long-term promissory notes, bank loans, and other obligations.

Bonds are carried on the balance sheet at their par value. Keep in mind that the actual market prices of the company's own bonds *could* be either at a premium (above par) or at a discount (below par). The coupon rate and maturity date are usually indicated for each bond outstanding. The liabilities section of the balance sheet of our typical manufacturing corporation looks like this:

Liabilities	
Accounts payable	$200,000
Accrued expenses	150,000
Accrued taxes	+ 50,000
Total current liabilities	$400,000
Convertible debentures	+500,000
8% interest, due 19Z5	
Total liabilities	$900,000

Shareholders' Equity

The difference between the corporation's total assets and total liabilities is referred to as *stockholders' equity* or net worth. The final section of the balance sheet therefore represents the stockholders' equity, which is the stake that the stockholders, both common and preferred, have in their corporation. This section itemizes the amount of equity or *ownership* of the *true owners* of the corporation, the shareholders. The items in this category are

1. Preferred stock
2. Common stock
3. Paid-in capital (capital surplus)

4. Retained earnings (earned surplus)

Preferred Stock. Like common stock, *preferred stock* is an equity security. Holders of such stock are considered to be owners of the corporation in contrast to bondholders who are considered creditors. Fittingly, preferred stock, which is ordinarily senior to common stock with respect to dividends and liquidation rights, is listed first. Such stock is carried *not* at its market value, but at its total par value, which in most instances is approximately equal to the amount the company received when the stock was first sold to the public. This listed figure usually approximates the amount that the preferred shareholders are entitled to receive if the company is dissolved. Most balance sheets detail information about any preferred stock listed, such as par value, convertibility (if any), dividend rate, and the number of shares authorized, issued, or outstanding.

Example:

Preferred stock	$75,000
6% Cumulative—$100 par	
Authorized, issued, and outstanding	
750 shares	

All 750 authorized shares of preferred stock are issued and outstanding.

750 Shares x $100 Par = $75,000 Book value
(Total par value)

Each share of $100 par preferred stock is entitled to a dividend at 6% of the par value each year. In other words, 6% of $100 equals a $6-per-share annual dividend. The balance sheet indicates that such dividends are cumulative. In the event that any preferred dividends are skipped, the company may not pay dividends on the common stock until all back dividends on the preferred stock (arrearages) have been paid.

Common Stock. The balance sheet shows the number of shares of common stock outstanding and their par value. At one time, par value represented the price at which the shares were first sold by the corporation, but that is no longer true. After the initial offering, par value has very little real significance. For our purposes, let's consider the amount shown on the balance sheet as common stock to represent the company's seed money—the amount of money, at *par value,* that the company first received from the sale of stock. In recent years, because stock transfer taxes are based on par values, corporations are assigning par value well below the price at which the shares are sold. Today, par value has little or no meaning in terms of the value of the shares.

Example:

Common stock $10 par	$300,000
Authorized, issued, and outstanding 30,000 shares	

Paid-In Capital. This item, also called *capital surplus,* shows the amount of money the company received from the sale of shares of common stock to the public *in addition* to the par value.

Example: Roxbury Manufacturing starts in business by selling 20,000 shares of stock at their original par value of $10 each. After this initial offering, the common stock section of the balance sheet shows $200,000. At least at this point in time, there is *no* paid-in capital. If, at a later date, the company issues another 10,000 shares at $20 each, the "extra" money received—the amount *over* par value—is indicated in the paid-in capital section of the balance sheet. The *basic* received ($10 par value) is added to the common stock account. The overage (the $10 which *exceeded* par value) goes into the paid-in capital account.

Common stock $10 par	$300,000
Authorized, issued, and outstanding 30,000 shares	
Paid-in capital (capital surplus)	100,000

This entry indicates that the owners of the business invested a total of $400,000 in common stock, of which $100,000 exceeded the total par value of $300,000. Generally, therefore, the *total* of these two accounts (common stock and paid-in capital) indicates the amount of money the company has received through the sale of its common stock to investors.

Retained Earnings. Also known as *earned surplus*, this section shows the amount of profit that the company retains in the business *after* paying any dividends on the common stock. In a sense, retained earnings represent profits that have not yet been paid out to the common stockholders in the form of dividends.

Example: A company is formed by selling a share of common stock at $100 per share to ten different people. The total amount collected is used to purchase goods at wholesale for subsequent resale. An early balance sheet is as follows:

Assets		*Liabilities*	
Inventory	$1,000		-0-
		Stockholders' Equity	
		Common stock $100 par	$1,000

At this point, total assets ($1,000 in inventory) equal total liabilities (zero) plus stockholders' equity ($1,000). The company then sells the inventory for a total of $2,000 and uses all the cash to purchase still more inventory.

Situation is now:

Assets		*Liabilities*	
Inventory	$1,000		-0-
		Stockholders' Equity	
		Common stock $100 par	$1,000
		Retained earnings	$1,000

The $1,000 earned profit, over and above its initial investment, appears in the retained earnings account.

The total of $2,000 under stockholders' equity, however, does not mean that the shareholders will receive $20 back for their $10 investments. These retained earnings are *not* cash: The profit has already been reinvested in additional inventory. Since the average balance sheet lists many items at *other than* their liquidation values, the chances of the shareholders' receiving cash equal to the net worth (shareholders' equity) portion of the balance sheet are small. Remember that shareholders' equity represents the amount that the stockholders *would* receive, *if* all assets were sold at the values at which they are carried on the balance sheet (book value), and *if* all liabilities were paid off at their balance sheet figures.

Example: A company is formed through the sale of 1,000 shares of preferred stock at $100 per share and 300,000 shares of common stock at $1 per share. It uses some of the cash received to purchase machinery and raw materials, but it does not pay for all the items in full. Our balance sheet looks like this:

Assets		*Liabilities*	
Cash	$160,000	Accounts payable	$ 50,000
Inventory	+ 85,000		
		Stockholders' Equity	
Total current assets	$245,000	Preferred stock $100 par	100,000
Property, plant, and equipment	+405,000	Common stock $1 par	+500,000
Total assets	$650,000	Total liabilities and stockholders' equity	$650,000

At this early period of the company's development, it has no profits and therefore no retained earnings. But it operates successfully over time and increases its assets by $200,000 through sales and its liabilities by only $50,000. The difference between the value of the newly acquired items and the additional debt—$150,000—represents a "gain" for the company's owners. At least in theory, the stockholders are "worth" $150,000 more, a profit shown as retained earnings. Keep in mind that the $150,000 thus "earned" is spread out among various assets. To realize this sum in cash, the company would have to liquidate some assets. The balance sheet now looks like that on the following page.

The balance sheet balances! If the company decides to liquidate, it realizes $850,000 in cash from the sale of the assets, at least in theory. If it next pays off all obligations ($100,000 for all liabilities), it would have a total of $750,000 (less taxes on gain) to be distributed to the owners of the company, its shareholders. The preferred stockholders are entitled to receive par for their stock ($100,000), leaving $650,000 for the common stockholders. The common-stockholders' stake in the company can be found by adding together the common stock listing ($500,000), paid-in capital ($0), and retained earnings ($150,000). The sum of these three figures shows the *common* stockholders' equity.

Assets		Liabilities	
Cash	$ 80,000	Accounts payable	$ 60,000
Accounts receivable	135,000	Accrued expenses	+ 40,000
Inventory	+140,000	Total liabilities	$100,000
Total current assets	$355,000	*Stockholders' Equity*	
Property, plant, and equipment	+470,000	Preferred stock $100 par	100,000
Prepaid expenses	+ 25,000	Common stock $1 par	500,000
		Retained earnings	+150,000
Total assets	$850,000	Total liabilities and stockholders' equity	$850,000

On the other hand, let us assume the company decides to continue operations for future profits. To reward the stockholders, it decides to distribute a dividend. Since the term *retained earnings* means earning retained in the business, any distributed earnings in the form of dividends *decreases* retained earnings.

BALANCE SHEET ANALYSIS

This section analyzes the balance sheet by looking at capitalization and book value. You have already compared current assets with current liabilities in the first section of this appendix.

Capitalization (Capital Structure–Invested Capital)

A company's *capitalization* is simply the sum of the balance sheet values for the corporation's bonds, preferred stock, and common stock. All *three* elements of the common stock are added: common stock, paid-in capital, and retained earnings. Thus, capitalization represents the money invested in the company by the *original* purchasers of the bonds, preferred stock, and common stock. It also reflects retained earnings, which is the capital that has *not* been paid out as dividends but that rather has been reinvested in the company. Capitalization thus tells us how a company got its funds and, secondarily, how it is handling them.

Capitalization is expressed in terms of three ratios, one each for bonds, common, and preferred stock. Each of these *capitalization ratios* represents the proportion of money collected through each vehicle to the *total* capitalization amount, assuming the total amount is equal to 100%.

In Table III–3, Roxbury's capitalization is shown to be $1,235,000, calculated as follows:

Bonds	+	Preferred stock	+	Common stock	+	Capital surplus	+	Retained earnings	=	Capitalization
$500,000	+	$75,000	+	$300,000	+	$100,000	+	$260,000	=	$1,235,000

The *bond ratio* is derived by dividing total capitalization into the funded debt, usually outstanding bonds maturing five years or more in the future.

$$\text{Bond ratio} = \frac{\text{Bonds}}{\text{Total capitalization}}$$

Example: See the balance sheet in Table III–3.

$$\text{Bond ratio} = \frac{\$500{,}000}{\$1{,}235{,}000} = 0.405 \text{ or } 40.5\%$$

The *preferred stock* ratio is found by dividing total capitalization into the par value of the preferred stock.

$$\text{Preferred stock ratio} = \frac{\text{Preferred stock}}{\text{Total capitalization}}$$

$$= \frac{\$75{,}000}{\$1{,}235{,}000} = 0.061 \text{ or } 6.1\%$$

The *common stock ratio* is found by dividing total capitalization into *all three parts* of the common stock account.

$$\text{Common stock ratio} = \frac{\text{Common stock} + \text{Capital surplus} + \text{Retained earnings}}{\text{Total capitalization}}$$

$$= \frac{\$300{,}000 + \$100{,}000 + \$260{,}000}{\$1{,}235{,}000} = 0.534 \text{ or } 53.4\%$$

All three capitalization ratios add up to 100%.

TABLE III–3.

BALANCE SHEET
ROXBURY MANUFACTURING COMPANY
December 31, 19Y3

Assets		*Liabilities*	
Cash	$ 75,000	Accounts payable	$ 200,000
Marketable securities	150,000	Accrued expenses	150,000
Accounts receivable	375,000	Accrued taxes	50,000
Inventory	400,000	Total current liabilities	$ 400,000
Total current assets	$1,000,000	Bonds—8%, due 19X5	500,000
Property, plant and equipment	$ 605,000	Total liabilities	$ 900,000
Prepayments	20,000		
Intangibles	10,000	*Stockholders' Equity*	
		Preferred stock—6% ($100 par)	$ 75,000
		Common stock ($10 par)	300,000
		Capital surplus	100,000
		Retained earnings	260,000
		Total stockholders' equity	$ 735,000
Total assets	$1,635,000	Total liabilities and stockholders' equity	$1,635,000

FIGURE III–2. Breakdown of Roxbury's Capitalization Ratios.

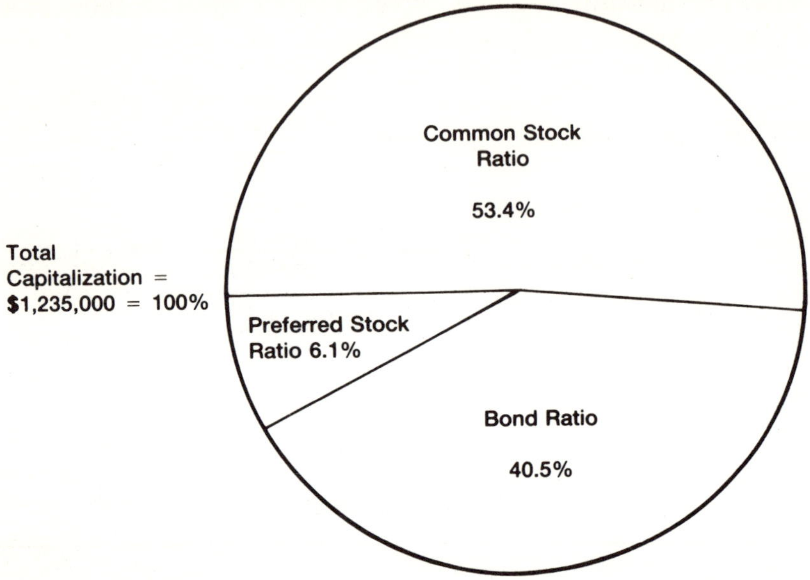

There are certain capitalization ratio yardsticks. For example, if the bond and preferred stock ratios combined exceed 33% of the total capitalization, an industrial company is generally considered by industry standards to have a highly leveraged capital structure. This condition may be considered speculative. Banks that use large amounts of borrowed money and public utilities that are very capital intensive will generally have debts far in excess of 50%. In this case, highly leveraged capitalization ratios are not speculative.

Book Value

The net tangible assets backing each share of common stock is known as *book value*. Calculating book value is easy. Since the balance sheet always shows the theoretical value of the common stockholders' equity (common stock + paid-in capital + retained earnings), just subtract the *intangibles* (if any) and divide by the number of outstanding common shares. The formula, applied to the sample balance sheet from the previous section on capitalization, is as follows:

Book Value	=	Common stock	+	Capital surplus	+	Retained earnings	−	Intangibles	÷	Number of share of common stock outstanding
	=	($300,000	+	$100,000	+	$260,000	−	$10,000)	÷	$30,000
	=	$21.67 per share								

The book value per common share represents the amount of cash that would be available for each share of common stock if all the assets (excepting intangibles) are sold *at the values at which they are carried on the balance sheet* and if all liabilities, bondholders, and preferred stockholders are also paid off. For our purposes, assume that the company must pay the bondholders and preferred stockholders the total par value of their securities as shown on the balance sheet. (However, accountants would most probably use the higher value between the total par value as shown on the balance sheet and the total market value based on the call price of their securities.)

A company's book value can be of great significance, despite the fact that, in the real world, liquidating the company at balance sheet values is virtually impossible. An increasing book value is generally considered to be a healthy sign for a company; a decreasing book value may indicate a weakening financial situation. To the securities analyst, whether a company's book value is *increasing* or *decreasing* is especially significant. While normally a company's *book value* and its *market value* bear no correlation (with some exceptions, mostly for financial service companies, such as insurance firms), these values do usually move in concert. Foe example, the bid shown in the newspaper for mutual funds is actually the book value of a share of the fund.

Summary Comment

The balance sheet reflects the company's financial position at a particular point in time—what it owns, what it owes, and what the shareholders are worth. It is like a snapshot of a subject "on the run"—the action is frozen, and the values are reflected as of the close of business on the balance sheet date.

While one balance sheet can be very revealing, a series of balance sheets, possibly covering the previous five or six years of operations, can be of even greater significance. The *trends* are extremely important. Is this year's current ratio better or worse than it has been over the last several years? Is the book value per common share going higher or lower? A study of the ratios *over a period of a few years* can reveal much about the company's future prospects.

INCOME STATEMENT

Construction

Corporate annual reports traditionally show a balance sheet representing the corporation's financial picture on a particular day, usually the final day of the company's fiscal year. Most annual reports contain another financial statement in addition to the balance sheet—the income statement. The *income statement* (also known as the *profit and loss statement*), a statement of income and expenses usually over the *entire* year, shows how much the company made or lost during the year. A typical, simplified, income statement appears in Table III–4. (Assume 30,000 shares of common stock outstanding.) Review that statement briefly before we examine it entry by entry.

Note: The tax rate used in these examples is 50%—for simplicity's sake. The tax rates may change but the principles of financial analysis remain the same.

Net Sales. The *net sales* listing shows the amount of money that the company took in as the result of its manufacturing activities. "Net" reflects the fact that returned goods and discounts have been taken into account. Were this a nonmanufacturing enterprise (such as an airline or utility), this item might be called *operating revenues.*

TABLE III–4.

STATEMENT OF INCOME
ROXBURY MANUFACTURING COMPANY
January 1–December 31, 19Y3

Net sales	$2,000,000
Cost of goods sold	–1,590,000
Selling, general, and administrative expenses	– 154,000
Depreciation	– 56,000
Operating income	$ 200,000
Other income	+ 7,500
Total income (EBIT)	$ 207,500
Interest on bonds	– 40,000
Taxes (50% rate)	– 83,750
Net income	83,750
Preferred dividends	– 4,500
Earnings available for common stock	$ 79,250

Cost of Goods Sold. Think of this item as "factory" costs. It includes such factors as the costs of maintaining the manufacturing facilities, raw materials, and labor.

Selling, General, and Administrative Expenses. This item includes the cost of running the *sales* office of the company: office payroll, salespersons' commissions, advertising, and other such nonmanufacturing expenses.

Depreciation. The annual depreciation of the fixed assets appears in this category. You may consider this a *noncash expense* because the assets may have been paid for long ago but are being "charged off" in small increments each year.

Operating Income. Subtracting the operating costs from net sales gives operating income. We call it operating income because it is "factory" profit, and we have not yet considered other investments, rents, royalties, or income from sources other than manufacturing.

Other Income. The income the company receives as dividends and/or interest on the marketable securities it may own appears here. This item may also include other sources of income not related directly to the firm's operations, such as the sale of real estate (above book value) or rental income or unused land held for future use.

Total Income. Also known as *earnings before interest and taxes* (EBIT), this category is self-explanatory.

Interest on Bonds. Almost as self-explanatory is the amount of money that the corporation pays out each year to service its outstanding bonds.

Taxes. Federal and state income taxes, for our purposes, can be figured at roughly 50%. Thus, 50% of ($207,500 – $40,000) gives us $83,750 in taxes. (The 50% rate has been eliminated by the Tax Reform Act of 1986, but it is kept here because representation of taxes on the income statement remains the same—and 50% is a simple calculation.)

Net Income. This item is also known as *net profit.* All income and all expenses have now been weighted against each other. Only the stockholders remain to be satisfied.

Preferred Dividends. Note that the corporation deducted its bond interest payments *before* figuring its tax liability. Preferred dividend payments, however, are *not* a deductible item and do not lower taxes.

Earnings Available for Common Stock. Some call these net earnings, because they may be reinvested in the company and/or paid out to the common stockholders as cash dividends. Any amount *not* paid out as dividends, at least in theory, increases the retained earnings accounts.

Analysis

Just as balance sheet ratios measure a company's financial strength, so too do important income statement ratios reflect a company's state of affairs. In the following analysis, use the income statement shown in Table III–4.

Expense Ratio (Operating Ratio). The *expense ratio,* also known as the *operating ratio,* is an excellent measure of corporate efficiency and should therefore be compared with the results of prior years. An increasing expense ratio could indicate a company's loss of control over cost.

$$\text{Expense ratio} = \frac{\text{Operating costs}}{\text{Net sales}}$$

$$\text{Expense ratio} = \frac{\text{Cost of goods sold + Selling, general, and administrative expenses + Depreciation}}{\text{Net sales}}$$

$$= \frac{\$1{,}590{,}000 + 154{,}000 + 56{,}000}{2{,}000{,}000} = 0.9 \text{ or } 90\%$$

Margin of Profit Ratio. The complement of the expense ratio, this ratio shows the percentage of the sales dollar *not* eaten up by operating costs. It is derived by dividing operating income by net sales.

$$\text{Margin of profit ratio} = \frac{\text{Operating income}}{\text{Net sales}}$$

$$= \frac{\$200{,}000}{2{,}000{,}000} = 0.10 \text{ or } 10\%$$

Note that the margin of profit ratio plus the operating ratio equals 100%.

Cash Flow. Realizing that one of the operating expenses—depreciation—is artificial, you might ask how much actual cash the company has available before it pays out any money on preferred or common stock cash dividends. Depreciation is not actually spent, at least not in the current year, and therefore cash flow is equal to the sum of net income and annual depreciation.

$$\text{Cash flow} = \text{Net income} + \text{Annual depreciation}$$
$$= \$83{,}750 + 56{,}000 = \$139{,}750$$

Interest Coverage. When examining a company you want to know how well it provides for the payment of interest on its outstanding bonds. To find out, divide total income (EBIT) by the interest on the bonds.

$$\text{Interest coverage} = \frac{\text{Total income (EBIT)}}{\text{Interest on bonds}}$$
$$= \frac{\$207{,}500}{\$40{,}000} = 5.2 \text{ times}$$

Interest coverage of over four times is usually considered a safe margin for the protection of a company.

Preferred Dividend Coverage. Another question is: How well are the preferred dividends covered by earnings? To find out, simply divide the net income by the preferred dividend requirements.

$$\text{Preferred dividend coverage} = \frac{\text{Net income}}{\text{Preferred dividends}}$$
$$= \frac{\$83{,}750}{\$4{,}500} = 18.6 \text{ times}$$

The calculation shows that the earnings cover the preferred dividends 18.6 times over.

Primary Earnings per Share. The earnings per share ratio is probably the most widely used measure of how well a company's fortunes are faring. As a result, it is also the most widely advertised measure—the bottom line. This most important measurement is determined by dividing the net earnings (which is equal to net income minus preferred dividends) by the number of common shares outstanding.

$$\text{Primary earnings per share} = \frac{\text{Net earnings}}{\text{Number of shares of common stock outstanding}}$$

$$= \frac{\$79{,}250}{30{,}000} = \$2.64$$

The expression "earnings per share" has practically been replaced by the more modern expression *primary earnings per share*. The newer term reflects earnings as they would be if all "common stock equivalents" were issued and outstanding as common stock, thus diluting "ordinary" earnings per share by 3% or more. Common stock equivalents include warrants, stock options, and *certain* convertible bonds and convertible preferred shares. Common stock equivalents, if they exist, are clearly labeled. Corporations now report primary earnings per share so that the investing public does *not* have to refigure the "ordinary" earnings per share. Nor does the public have to determine which convertible items are considered common stock equivalents. When earnings are figured to include *all* possible additional shares of common stock, whether common stock equivalents or not, then such earnings are reported as "fully diluted."

Fully Diluted Earnings per Share. A corporation may have convertible bonds and/or convertible preferred stock outstanding. Investors realize that earnings per common share would be affected if such securities were to be converted. Fully diluted earnings reflect the per-share results as they *would* be if all *potential* common shares were added to the outstanding common stock. Under this method all warrants, stock options (options issued *privately* by the corporation), and convertible issues are considered as exchanged for additional common stock.

It is beyond the scope of this text to determine which common stock equivalents are included in the primary earnings per share and which are reserved for fully diluted earnings. Suffice it to say that fully diluted means just what it says: All potential common shares are included.

Table III–5 contains the same basic figures as those in Table III–4, but they have been recalculated on the assumption that the outstanding bonds are convertible and that they *have been* converted. The bonds are convertible into 20,000 additional shares of stock, and, again, the corporate tax rate is 50%. Assuming that the convertible bonds are exchanged for common stock, the interest on bonds entry disappears. With the deduction of $40,000 gone, the income *before* tax rises from $167,500 to $207,500. At a tax rate of 50%, the tax burden under fully diluted conditions is $103,750 instead of $83,750, thus *raising* net earnings from $79,250 to $99,250. Again assuming that the bonds are converted, we must take into account the additional shares thus created. If 30,000 shares were outstanding before the conversion, then the fully diluted earnings figure is calculated by dividing the "new" net earnings by 50,000 shares of common stock (30,000 outstanding + 20,000 after conversion). Of course, all these changes affect the "ordinary" earnings per share of the corporation.

$$\text{Fully diluted earnings per share} = \frac{\text{Earnings available for common stock}}{\text{Number of shares of common stock outstanding after conversion}}$$

$$= \frac{\$99{,}250}{50{,}000} = \$1.99$$

TABLE III–5.

STATEMENT OF INCOME
(Fully Diluted)
ROXBURY MANUFACTURING COMPANY
January 1–December 31, 19Y3

Net sales	$2,000,000
Cost of goods sold	–1,590,000
Selling, general, and administrative expenses	– 154,000
Depreciation	– 56,000
Operating income	$ 200,000
Other income	+ 7,500
Total income (EBIT)	$ 207,500
Taxes (39% rate)	– 103,750
Net income	103,750
Preferred dividends	– 4,500
Earnings available for common stock	$ 99,250

OTHER ANALYSES

Payout Ratio

Most corporations pay out at least a part of their net earnings to common shareholders through cash dividends. The percentage of earnings so distributed is known as the *payout ratio*. As a rough guideline, growth companies may be expected to have low payout ratios (10%), compared with a typical manufacturing company payout of approximately 50%. This ratio is derived by dividing the total common dividends paid by the total net earnings, which is net income minus preferred dividends.

$$\text{Payout ratio} = \frac{\text{Common stock dividends}}{\text{Net income} - \text{Preferred dividends}}$$

Example: A corporation with $1,000,000 in net income pays $50,000 in preferred dividends and $375,000 in common stock dividends. Its payout ratio is

$$\text{Payout ratio} = \frac{\$375{,}000}{\$1{,}000{,}000 - \$50{,}000} = 0.395 \text{ or } 39.5\%$$

Yield on Common Stock

To determine *current yield,* divide a security's annual dividends (or interest) by its current market price.

$$\text{Current yield} = \frac{\text{Annual dividend rate}}{\text{Market price}}$$

Generally speaking, companies with greater prospects for growth have lower yields, because growth companies usually reinvest most of their earnings in their own businesses.

Example: A common stock has a current market price of 42 and pays annual dividends of $1.80. Its current yield is 4.3%, calculated thus:

$$\text{Current yield} = \frac{\$1.80}{\$42} = 0.043 \text{ or } 4.3\%$$

Inventory Turnover Ratio

We can measure how effectively the company is selling its products by determining how often its supply of inventory is manufactured and sold. Of the several methods for calculating this ratio, the simplest (and least accurate) is as follows:

$$\text{Inventory turnover ratio} = \frac{\text{Net sales}}{\text{Year-end inventory}}$$

This method is presented because it is simple and workable. Other methods use the cost of goods sold rather than net sales, as the numerator and the *average* inventory, rather than year-end inventory, as the denominator. As a general guide, a good inventory turnover ratio for an average manufacturing company is six times per year.

Example: A corporation's annual report shows net sales of $14,000,000 (on the income statement) and an inventory of $2,682,000 (on the balance sheet). The inventory turnover is 5.2 times, determined as follows:

$$\text{Inventory turnover ratio} = \frac{\$14{,}000{,}000}{\$2{,}682{,}000} = 5.2 \text{ times}$$

Price-Earnings Ratio

The *price-earnings* (P/E) ratio is one of the most significant measurements. It is also called the price multiple. It relates a corporation's profitability to the market price of its common shares, thus affording a measure of the *relative* expensiveness of the common stock. Typically, growth stocks have high P/E ratios; companies with poorer prospects sell at lower earnings multiples. To obtain this ratio, divide the market price of the company's common stock by the earnings per share.

$$\text{Price-earnings ratio} = \frac{\text{Current market price of the common stock}}{\text{Common stock earnings per share}}$$

Example: Company A earned $1.04 per share. Its common stock is selling in the open market at 23 1/4.

$$\text{Price-earnings (P/E) ratio} = \frac{\$23.25}{\$1.04} = 22.4$$

Each share of common stock is selling for about 22 times the amount of earnings generated by each share.

Return on Equity

An informative measure of management's efficiency is the *return on equity,* derived by dividing net income by shareholders' equity. (Shareholders' equity is the sum of preferred stock, common stock, paid-in capital, and retained earnings.)

$$\text{Return on equity} = \frac{\text{Net income}}{\text{Shareholders' equity}}$$

Example: Refer to Tables III–3 and III–4. For a corporation with net income of $83,750 and shareholders' equity of $735,000:

$$\text{Return on equity} = \frac{\$83{,}750}{\$735{,}000} = 0.114 \text{ or } 11.4\%$$

Return on Invested Capital

A measure of how well the company is utilizing its entire capitalization is the *return on invested capital.* The formula is

$$\text{Return on invested capital} = \frac{\text{Net income + Interest on debt}}{\text{Total capitalization (invested capital)}}$$

Example: Again using the balance sheet and the income statement in Tables III–3 and III–4, you can calculate the interest on bonds ($40,000) by multiplying the coupon rate, 8%, by the total par value, $500,000. After that, simply fill in the formula:

$$\text{Return on invested capital} = \frac{\$83{,}750 + \$40{,}000}{\$1{,}235{,}000}$$

$$= 10.0\%$$

"Financial Reasoning" Problems

Let us apply our knowledge of accounting by following the effects of a managerial decision on the corporation's financial statements. In each instance, we shall trace the course of events, noting the impact on the company's assets, liabilities, shareholders' equity, and several of the more common ratios.

Stock Splits. When a common stock is split, the *number of shares* of common stock *increases* and the *par value* of the common stock *decreases* in the same proportion.

Example: A "beginning" common shareholders' equity before a split consists of:

Common stock: at $.40 par value, 600,000 shares authorized, 300,000 shares issued and outstanding	$120,000
Paid-in capital	40,000
Retained earnings	+135,000
Total common stockholders' equity	$295,000

In a 2-for-1 split, the number of issued and outstanding shares doubles (from 300,000 to 600,000) and the par value is halved (from $.40 to $.20). The *new* common stockholders' equity looks like this after the split:

Common stock: at $.20 par value, 600,000 shares authorized, 600,000 shares issued and outstanding	$120,000
Paid-in capital	40,000
Retained earnings	+135,000
Total common stockholders' equity	$295,000

Because of the 2-for-1 split, the par value changes from $.40 to $.20 but the number of outstanding shares doubles. No *real* change occurs in the balance sheet. The common stock account *still* comes out to $120,000:

300,000 shares @ $.40 par = $120,000 *and*

600,000 shares @ $.20 par = $120,000

Certainly a greater number of shares are outstanding; but, at least in theory, the shareholders are no better off (and no *worse* off) than they were before the split. Traditionally a flurry of buying follows a stock split. The market theory is that the stock will sell better at a lower price after the split because it is more marketable. People tend to favor lower-priced issues even though a lower-priced security bears no more intrinsic value than a higher-priced security. The actual net effect of the split is nil, because the book values on the balance sheet do not change.

Stock Dividends. Stock dividends result in the issuance of additional shares, but the par value of the common stock does *not* change.

Example: Using the same stockholders' equity statement from the previous section, let us restate the figures as they appear after the payment of a 30% stock dividend, that is, 90,000 shares (30% of 300,000):

Common stock: at $.40 par value, 600,000 shares authorized, 390,000 shares issued and outstanding	$156,000
Paid-in capital	40,000
Retained earnings	+ 99,000
Total common stockholders' equity	$295,000

Compare the previous figures with these. The *total* equity does not change. Nevertheless, the common stock account increases by $36,000 (from $120,000 to $156,000), and the retained earnings account decreases by $36,000 (from $135,000 to $99,000). Our common stockholders are no richer or poorer, but the balance sheet changes in that the common stock account increases at the expense of the retained earnings account.

Smaller stock dividends (generally less than 23%) are treated differently. Paid-in capital may also be increased, and the market value of the common stock may be taken into account.

Declaration of Cash Dividends. For the remainder of this section use the balance sheet in Table III–6.

A board of directors announces a cash dividend payment of $0.50 per common share approximately two months before the dividends are actually paid out to the stockholders. As a result, the Doktabessie Corporation balance sheet undergoes changes between the time the corporation declares a cash dividend and the time it actually pays it.

The declaration of a cash dividend creates a current liability of $6,000 ($0.50 x 12,000 common shares). Current liabilities must be adjusted to include this *new* obligation, which must be paid out within the next year. An item (probably labeled "dividends payable") is added to current liabilities, raising the total by $6,000 to $477,000. Where does this $6,000 come from? From the accumulated retained earnings! As you will recall, retained earnings may be thought of as unpaid dividends. Management has now decided to pay some of this accumulated value to the common stockholders. So we now *reduce* retained earnings by $6,000 (from $290,000 to $284,000). The overall change on the balance sheet is an increase in current liabilities and a decrease in retained earnings.

Since current assets remain the same while current liabilities have increased, several ratios are adversely affected. The dividend reduces the:

- Working capital (net current assets)

TABLE III–6.

DOKTABESSIE CORPORATION
BALANCE SHEET
June 30, 19Y3

Assets		*Liabilities*	
Cash	$ 165,000	Accounts payable	$166,000
Marketable securities	18,000	Accrued taxes	70,000
Accounts receivable	260,000	Notes payable	84,000
Inventory	455,000	Accrued expenses	151,000
Total current assets	$ 898,000	*Total current liabilities*	$471,000
		First mortgage bonds: 7 1/2% due 1/1/ZA	500,000
		Total liabilities	$971,000
Property, plant, and equipment:		*Stockholders' Equity*	
Land	$ 75,000	Preferred stock ($100 par, 1,000 shares authorized, issued, and outstanding)	100,000
Buildings	506,000		
Equipment	89,000		
Machinery	164,000		
	834,000	Common stock ($25 par, 12,000 shares authorized, issued, and outstanding)	300,000
Less: Accumulated depreciation	– 217,000		
Net property, plant, and equipment	$ 617,000	Paid-in capital	58,000
Intangibles	204,000	Accumulated retained earnings	290,000
Total assets	$1,719,000	*Total stockholders' equity*	748,000
		Total liabilities and stockholders' equity	$1,719,000

- Quick asset ratio (acid test ratio)
- Current ratio

Logically, the dividend also reduces the common stockholders' stake in the company, because part of their accumulated profits is paid out to them. Understandably, the value remaining after they receive their dividends is reduced by the amount of such dividends.

Payment of Cash Dividends. When the Doktabessie Corporation actually pays out the cash dividends, the company is dispensing cash in the amount of the current liability established for such payment. The following changes occur:

- *Cash* decreases and
- *Dividends payable* disappears

Cash is now $159,000 ($165,000 – $6,000), and total current assets decreases to $892,000. The total current liabilities entry goes back to $471,000. Note where the *ultimate* change occurs: Cash is reduced, and the payment comes from retained earnings. The shift was done in two stages:

1. When the dividend is *declared,* retained earnings decrease and current liabilities increase.
2. When the dividend is *paid,* cash decreases and that particular current liability disappears.

Retiring Debt at a Discount. If the corporation's bonds are trading in the open market at a discount, the management may possibly elect to buy them back. Thus they can retire the obligation at a bargain rate rather than pay the holders full par value at maturity.

The Doktabessie Corporation buys $50,000 of its own bonds in the open market for a total of $40,000. The balance sheet changes as follows:

- Cash decreases by $40,000.
- Total current assets and *total* assets also decrease by the same amount.
- Working capital, quick assets, current ratio, and acid test (quick asset) ratio all decline because current assets are reduced while current liabilities remain unchanged.
- Bonds are reduced by $50,000.
- Stockholders' equity *increases* by $10,000 because we have reduced assets (cash) by $40,000 and liabilities by $50,000. Thus we gain $10,000, which is reflected in increased net

worth. Since the company has "paid off" a $50,000 debt at a cost of only $40,000, the stockholders have gained.

While the *cash* picture is not as good as it was and although some ratios have declined, the overall effect is good in that the stockholders' equity increases.

Retiring Debt at a Premium. The Doktabessie Corporation elects to retire some of its bonds through the exercise of a call provision. An early price is usually above par, so our corporation is paying a premium price for the early retirement of part of its debt. Calling $100,000 par value of bonds at a price of 102 ($1,020 per bond) costs the corporation $102,000. The management is eliminating a $100,000 debt (liabilities), but the cost is $102,000 in cash (assets). It pays the extra $2,000 from retained earnings.

Note the effects on the corporation's balance sheet. Cash decreases from $165,000 to $63,000. Current assets, of course, now total only $796,000 and total assets, $1,617,000. On the liabilities side of the balance sheet, the bonds go down from $500,000 to $400,000 and total liabilities from $971,000 to $871,000. Retained earnings reflect the $2,000 "loss" the company suffered and decreases from $292,000 to $288,000. The new balance sheet shows:

Total assets	=	Total liabilities	+	Net worth (Stockholders' equity)
$1,617,000	=	871,000	+	746,000

The cash spent also adversely affects working capital, current ratio, quick assets, and the liquidity (quick asset) ratio.

Sale and Lease-Back of Fixed Assets. The Doktabessie Corporation decides to raise cash by selling and leasing back some of its expensive machinery. The corporation sells machinery carried on its balance sheet at $30,000. This sale reduces the property, plant, and equipment from $617,000 to $587,000. At the same time it increases current assets from $898,000 to $928,000 because cash goes up to $195,000.

The effect on the balance sheet depends on whether the sale is made at a price greater or lower than the value at which the assets are carried on the balance sheet. Essentially, if the sale is made for more than the book value of the asset, the corporation makes a "profit." For sales of assets at prices below their book value, the corporation sustains a "loss." In essence, the company is exchanging a *fixed* asset (machinery) for a *current* asset (cash). This shift increases current assets at the expense of fixed assets and thus improves working capital and the current ratio. Since current assets increase while the current liabilities remain the same, the corporation's working capital increases (current assets – current liabilities). The current ratio (current assets ÷ current liabilities) also improves. In short:

- *If the asset is sold at a profit, total* assets increase, and the increase is also reflected in the retained earnings account.
- *If the asset is sold at a loss, total* assets decrease (by the difference between the book value and the sale price of the asset sold). The decrease also lowers the retained earnings account by the same amount.

CONCLUDING COMMENTS

This appendix explains, in simple fashion, the construction of the two most basic financial statements, the balance sheet and the income statement. You should now understand the basic purpose of each document and be able to examine such statements with an eye toward evaluating a company's future prospects.

These documents detail a corporation's financial position and its earnings. They show the end result of the management's efforts to run a profitable business. Knowing how to interpret this information is absolutely essential to a professional analysis of the company—the key ingredient to enable you to decide whether to buy or sell the company's securities.

APPENDIX **IV**

Obtaining Redress If You Feel You Have Been Defrauded

DEAL WITH THE COMPLIANCE DEPARTMENT

The majority of brokerage firms have compliance departments, which function as internal auditors. The compliance department is charged with the overall supervision of a firm's branch offices and branch managers and should know if a particular branch is poorly supervised and/or if its employees act in a dishonest manner. If you have a problem, the final level of appeal within a firm is to the compliance and/or legal departments.

WHERE TO TURN FOR HELP

Most problems and difficulties between registered representatives and customers are resolved internally. However, Congress, the various states, and the NASD provide additional means for customers who feel they have been treated unfairly to seek redress. The NASD and the legal authorities want to know if the management of a public company uses its position to steal from the company, if individuals profit from using "insider information" about impending corporate developments, and/or if any organized attempt is made to manipulate the price of a company's stock. In this section, we describe the various protections and defenses available to you as an individual investor and how to use them to assert your rights.

One of the first places individual investors consider turning in the event of difficulties with a registered rep or a brokerage firm is to the *Securities & Exchange Commission* (SEC). The name of the SEC appears almost daily in the financial press in connection with actions against public corporations or brokerage firms. (The number of such actions is small, however, considering how many public companies and securities firms are operating today, and the number of people employed in the business.)

How Can the SEC Assist the Individual Investor Seeking to Redress a Wrong?

Most problems are presented to the SEC either in the form of a letter or a personal meeting between the investor and the SEC's representative. In many ways a letter is the best approach because it allows you to describe what occurred in your own words and in a logical and coherent manner. When sending such a letter, you should include *copies* of any correspondence, confirmations, or documents in your possession that relate to the transaction in question. (Always keep your originals in a safe place—you may need them.) On receipt of such a letter or after a complaint is presented in person, the SEC must determine if the federal securities laws have been violated. In making this determination, the SEC consults all parties involved in the transaction—the registered rep as well as the customer. Many disputes between registered reps, the firms who employ them, and their customers are resolved at this level. Most complaints involving transaction errors or failure to deliver securities or dividends are also resolved here. If it can be shown that the firm or the particular account executive has a pattern of dishonest and illegal activity, the

SEC may bar the individual and/or the firm from the securities business and refer the matter to the U.S. Attorney's office for criminal prosecution.

Can the SEC Recover Money for an Individual Investor Who Has Been Defrauded?

The answer to this question is no. The SEC is not a collection agency. However, an SEC action against a registered rep, a brokerage firm, or a public corporation can be used as the basis for a civil suit brought by the wronged investor. In instances where well-known brokerage firms are the subject of SEC action, the firms generally seek to make good to the investors, if for no other reason than to reduce the bad publicity that accompanies SEC action.

State authorities play a role similar to that of the SEC. The effectiveness of state securities authorities varies considerably from one state to another as well as from one administration to another. The state authorities use their power to regulate limited partnerships set up as tax shelters, or for specific purposes (such as to raise money to finance a Broadway show). Many state authorities actively pursue the promoters of con schemes worked on the residents of a particular state or locale. The state and local authorities work closely with the federal authorities in seeking to eliminate the "bad apples" from the securities business. Like the SEC, state authorities are not empowered to represent individual investors nor to recover money on behalf of such investors.

HOW TO RECOVER YOUR MONEY

If federal and state authorities cannot recover money you lost to a con artist or crooked brokerage firm, *what can you do to get your money back?* Two basic mechanisms exist: arbitration and the use of private counsel.

Arbitration

Disciplinary action against a brokerage firm can be initiated with the NASD, as described in Appendix II. Within the past few years, the NASD has adopted a simplified uniform procedure for the processing and handling of cases in which investors seek to recover money from brokerage firms. The arbitration procedure comes into play when the claim against the brokerage firm is for $5,000 or less.

What Steps Must You Take to Initiate an Arbitration Procedure? Three steps are involved in starting an arbitration procedure. First, you must file with the arbitration authority—for OTC transactions, the NASD—a typewritten or printed letter describing the nature of the claim. Second, you must deposit with the arbitration authority a check or money order, in an amount prescribed by Section 2(c) of the Uniform Code of Arbitration. This requirement is intended to eliminate frivolous complaints; the final disposition of the deposit is left to the ruling of the arbitrator. Third, the complainant must sign and return to the authorities a submission agreement, stating that the complainant will submit to the jurisdiction of the arbitration authority and will accept the decision it reaches.

The arbitration process itself is relatively straightforward. The arbitration authority appoints an arbitrator (usually an individual who is not associated with or employed by a brokerage firm or securities industry association) to look into the matter. The arbitrator examines the claim submitted by the individual investor and determines if the matter can be resolved to the satisfaction of all parties involved without going to an actual hearing. The complainant has the right to insist on an actual arbitration hearing; but in many cases the mere presence of an impartial arbitrator results in settlement without a hearing.

If the complainant requests it, or the arbitrator feels that the matter cannot be resolved on the basis of the letter and the submitted documents, a date will be set for a formal arbitration hearing. This hearing is similar to a regular court procedure: The arbitrator and witnesses are sworn in, and each party is given the opportunity to make an opening statement. The individual making the complaint presents a case using the relevant documents and the testimony of live witnesses, and the parties that are the subject of the complaint are allowed to present their side of the case. Counterclaims and closing statements conclude the arbitration proceeding. After all the facts have been presented, the arbitrator reviews the whole matter, reaches a decision, and advises the disputing parties of the decision by mail. The arbitrator is empowered to order a brokerage firm to return money to an individual investor; and any decision is final as provided in the submission agreement.

This arbitration procedure has worked well when it involved a brokerage firm that was registered with the relevant authorities and a member of the Securities Industry Association. However, if the individual or firm is a fly-by-night operation without any fixed location or address, it is virtually impossible to use this procedure to recover money. Therefore, you *must* check out individual salespersons and the firms that employ them before you enter into any transactions.

Private Counsel

If more than $5,000 are involved in a dispute, or if you feel that a court of law would provide a better forum for your case, you can retain legal counsel and use the registered rep and the firm involved in the transaction. In recent years, a number of individual investors have brought such suits successfully and have been awarded large sums of money. The successful suits have had certain elements in common: First, the investors involved were able to show that they were relatively unsophisticated in the area of investing and that the trades in question were the first ones they entered into. The investors were also able to show that the disputed investments were totally inappropriate or excessive, considering the investors' ages or financial circumstances. For example, a court of law might find high-risk growth stocks or active option trading using complex strategies to be inappropriate investments for someone 85 years old. Many successful suits have shown that the registered rep used excessive influence in dealing with an older or infirm customer. But even in the most blatant instances, the costs of bringing such suits are high, and the party bringing the suit has no guarantee of success.

FINAL COMMENTS

As noted earlier, most disputes investors have with their registered reps and brokerage firms relate to errors or mistakes in the execution of trades. Many of these complaints stem from mismatches between the personality and philosophy of the customer and those of the registered reps or the brokerage firm. The majority of these complaints, however, can be easily resolved. If you feel uncomfortable with or distrust a particular registered rep, the wise move is to look for another registered rep with whom you are more comfortable. Changing registered reps is an easy process.

SOURCES FOR ADDITIONAL INFORMATION ON BROKERAGE FIRMS

- U.S. Securities and Exchange Commission, Public Reference Room, Washington, DC 20549, (202) 272-7450. Order a copy of a brokerage firm's registration statement (Form BD).
- U.S. Securities and Exchange Commission, Office of Consumer Affairs and Information Services, Washington, DC 20549, (202) 272-7440. "Consumers Should Know" booklet, "Investigate Before You Invest" booklet, "How to Proceed with the Arbitration of a Small Claim" booklet.

Regional and Branch Offices

- Region 1
NEW YORK REGIONAL OFFICE, 26 Federal Plaza, Room 1028, New York, NY 10278, (212) 264-1636. Region: New York and New Jersey.
- Region 2
BOSTON REGIONAL OFFICE, 150 Causeway St., Boston, MA 02144, (617) 223-2721. Region: Maine, New Hampshire, Vermont, Massachusetts, Rhode Island, Connecticut.
- Region 3
ATLANTA REGIONAL OFFICE, 1375 Peachtree St., NE, Suite 788, Atlanta, GA 30367, (404) 347-4768. Region: Tennessee, Virgin Islands, Puerto Rico, North Carolina, South Carolina, Georgia, Alabama, Mississippi, Florida, and Louisiana east of the Atchafalaya River.
- MIAMI BRANCH OFFICE, Dupont Plaza Center, 300 Biscayne Blvd. Way, Suite 500, Miami, FL 33131, (305) 350-5765.
- Region 4
CHICAGO REGIONAL OFFICE, Everett McKinley Dirksen Blvd., 219 South Dearborn St., Room 1204, Chicago, IL 60604, (312) 353-7390. Region: Michigan, Ohio, Kentucky, Wisconsin, Indiana, Iowa, Illinois, Minnesota, and Missouri.
- DETROIT BRANCH OFFICE, 231 W. Lafayette, 438 Federal Bldg. and U.S. Courthouse, Detroit, MI 48226, (313) 226-6070.
- Region 5
FORT WORTH REGIONAL OFFICE, 411 W. Seventh St., 8th Floor, Fort Worth, TX 76102, (817) 334-3821. Region: Oklahoma, Arkansas, Texas, and Louisiana west of the Atchafalaya River and Kansas.
- HOUSTON BRANCH OFFICE, 7500 San Felipe St., Suite 550, Houston, TX 77063, (713) 266-3671.

- Region 6
  DENVER REGIONAL OFFICE, 410 17th St., Suite 700, Denver, CO 80202, (303) 844-2071. Region: North Dakota, South Dakota, Wyoming, Nebraska, Colorado, New Mexico, and Utah.
- SALT LAKE BRANCH OFFICE, U.S. Post Office and Courthouse, 350 S. Main St., Room 505, Salt Lake City, UT 84101, (801) 524-5796.
- Region 7
  LOS ANGELES REGIONAL OFFICE, 5757 Wilshire Blvd., Suite 500 East, Los Angeles, CA 90036-3648, (213) 468-3098. Region: Nevada, Arizona, California, Hawaii, and Guam.
- SAN FRANCISCO BRANCH OFFICE, 450 Golden Gate Ave., Box 36042, San Francisco, CA 94102, (415) 556-5264.
- Region 8
  SEATTLE REGIONAL OFFICE, 3040 Jackson Federal Building, 915 Second Avenue, Seattle, WA 98174, (206) 442-7990. Region: Montana, Idaho, Washington, Oregon, and Alaska.
- Region 9
  PHILADELPHIA REGIONAL OFFICE, 600 Arch Street, Room 2204, Philadelphia, PA 19106, (215) 597-3100. Region: Pennsylvania, Delaware, Maryland, Virginia, West Virginia, and District of Columbia.

- The National Association of Securities Dealers, 1735 K Street, N.W., Washington, DC 20006, (202) 728-8000 (for over-the-counter securities).

- Municipal Securities Rulemaking Board, 1150 Connecticut Avenue, N.W., Suite 507, Washington, DC 20036, (202) 223-9347 (for municipal bonds).

C

T